THE LANGUAGE OF SOCIOLOGY

CHARLES W. LACHENMEYER

THE LANGUAGE
OF
SOCIOLOGY

 COLUMBIA UNIVERSITY PRESS

New York & London

Charles W. Lachenmeyer is Assistant Professor
of Sociology at Hunter College.

Copyright © 1971 Columbia University Press
Library of Congress Catalog Card Number: 72-164501
ISBN: 0-231-3556-X
Printed in the United States of America
10 9 8 7 6 5 4 3 2

Preface

AS AN UNDERGRADUATE major in sociology I felt a vague intellectual strain in trying to make sociology relevant to the things I observed about me. While stimulated by the "greats," I remember being puzzled by sociology's lack of power to explain the observable behavior of men. In my day-to-day affairs I would try to apply the general concepts I had inculcated, but to no avail: every explanation engendered a counterexplanation, every concept a rival. In graduate school this interest developed into a full-blown pursuit of an answer to the question, "Why does sociology fail to help me understand the observable social behavior of men?" My training was heavily statistical and methodological. Certainly sociologists were capable of recording the behavior of men and of attaching numbers to the categories that comprise these records: they had measures of the behavior of men. But these statistical indices struck me as being too far removed from the observable social behavior of men to be the basis of explanations of that behavior.

I turned to behaviorism for an adequate translation of sociological theory, but this detour was of limited utility. At the outset I rebelled at the fluidity and adaptability of the behaviorist language system. It was omnipotent in its ability to translate any sociological term or statement. I have always questioned anything that appears to be omnipotent and a review of a rather badly written paper of mine from an editor of *Sociometry* focused my objections. The paper was meant as a behavioristic translation of all social scientific theory about the etiology of mental illness. The editor rejected the paper, saying that such a translation without empirical support was just more debris in an already badly cluttered subdiscipline. Fortuitously, I had also just run across Chomsky's (1959) now famous review of Skinner's *Verbal Behavior* (1958). The general message of this review is that behavioristic "theory" is generalized beyond its real empirical limits.

Two further conclusions ended my hopeful exploration of behaviorism. One was that I came to regard the approach and its proponents as rejecting too many genuinely important questions and criticisms. Second, social behavior—to me a significant portion of the human behavioral domain—was treated inadequately. It struck me as methodological naiveté to measure and observe social behavior while excluding verbal behavior from the experiment.

Disappointed, I turned to the comforting concreteness of linguistics and the intellectual stimulation of semiotics, thinking that the key to an analysis of social behavior might be found in the study of verbal behavior. Linguistics proved to include much emphasis on what was to me irrelevant detail. The wider perspective of language as the core medium of social behavior was not to be found. Semiotics professed a wide perspective and mode of analysis. Yet, this proved to be more intention than empirical truth. The field had a name and a broad focus but too little substance to be of help in my pursuit.

I then turned to the philosophy of science to learn where I had gone wrong. If I could not find a discipline that answered my question, then maybe I could find a metadiscipline that could direct me to the formulation of such a discipline. If no discipline is available, one must be constructed; and where better to start than with the formulation of its logical foundations? This inquiry helped immensely to place many aspects of sociology, psychology, and social science in general in critical perspective.

This book is an outgrowth of that work. It is a critique of sociology based on gleanings from all the areas I have mentioned and some others as well, integrated by this last inquiry into the philosophy of science. It is the product of a sincere and costly effort to resolve the original question, and it does suggest several positive answers to this question in an analysis that, frankly, is so far logical rather than empirical.

Beside the intellectual debts acknowledged in references, I must express appreciation to my wife who, as a social psychologist, edited the final draft of the manuscript and clarified many of the arguments. She also took care of the technical details of having it typed and (as a superb cook) keeping me well fed in the interim. Mrs. Elizabeth Beck did an excellent and efficient job of typing both the rough draft and subsequent revisions. Finally, the staff of Columbia University Press have been exemplary.

CHARLES W. LACHENMEYER

Contents

THE LANGUAGE OF SOCIOLOGY

Introduction: An Overview

SOCIOLOGY IS NOT a science. Any science can be conceptualized as a dual information transfer. The first information transfer is between men and the events that are the subject matter of their science. The second is between men as scientists about these events. The success of this dual process is contingent on the adequacy of the special medium of the information transfer. This medium consists of linguistic and mathematical symbols which comprise a theory language. Sociology is not a science because its theory language is inadequate, and therefore the dual information transfer is inadequate.

This inadequacy has two separate but related manifestations. First, sociologists use terms and theoretical statements that are imprecise because they abound in ambiguity, vagueness, opacity, and contradiction: their terms and theoretical statements discriminate too wide a range of referents, too nebulous a range of referents, no true referents, or logically inconsistent referents. Second, and relatedly, sociologists often do not deal with observable phenomena but rather with reports about these phenomena or inferences based on these phenomena. Perhaps more important is the general failure of sociologists to replicate their investigations of any phenomena. In the case in which these phenomena are inferences or reports, the failure of replication is double jeopardy.

Sociology's present nonscientific status, due to these inadequacies, does not necessarily imply that sociology cannot become a science. However, such a transition has rather strict demands. First, sociologists must increase the precision of their theory language. Second, their investigative techniques can vary, but they should deal with observable phenomena. Short of this, they can study reports about behavior and inferential entities, provided they specify precise relationships between these phenomena and observable phenomena. In either case, they must replicate their research.

This book will attempt to explicate exhaustively this argument. The basic presentation relies heavily on some rather technical analyses. It is necessary first to specify the parameters of sociology.

As any sociologist knows, it is getting progressively more difficult, if in fact it was ever easy, to write a book about sociology. The field is divided into so many specialities that generalization is often impossible. This is true with respect to the phenomena studied: there are small groups men, organizations men, ecological adherents; there are sociologies of religion, crime, deviance, politics, economics, the arts, etc. Sociology as a logico-deductive enterprise can, however, be generalized about. There are uniformities among all sociologists in their approaches to constructing theories about the diverse phenomena they study. These uniformities are reflected in the basic assumptions of sociologists, in their core language for theory, in the range of research techniques they employ, and finally in the most fundamental unit of analysis with which they deal: social behavior. I shall consider each of these in turn in order to specify the parameters of the amorphous discipline of sociology of which this book will be a critique.

The Assumptions of Sociology

Sociologists consider their endeavors legitimate. That is, they believe that if one is a sociologist, he is a member of a professional group whose collective purpose is to progressively contribute to and improve a theoretically fruitful and pragmatically useful body of knowledge. This belief of legitimacy requires certain component statements that stand halfway between assumption and fact.

First of all, sociology has a valid subject matter. The definitions of this subject matter vary considerably, as examination of introductory texts reveals, and many sociologists would be hard pressed to identify its attributes, whatever the specialty with which they are concerned. However, whether implicitly or explicitly held, this assumption gives meaning to the sociologist's career and work.

Second, this subject matter can be described within certain tolerable limits of precision. This, in turn, implies several things. The sociologist can discriminate reliable units of analysis with specifiable spatio-temporal referents. Moreover, he can observe these units of analysis and assign them measurable values. The possibility exists, then, of developing measuring instruments with which to record these values within tolerable limits of error. He also has access to an adequate symbolic system, either mathematical or linguistic, with which to codify these descriptions and measurements. This is to say, a language system exists with which one sociologist can adequately communicate these descriptions and measurements to another sociologist.

The third assumption buttressing the legitimacy of sociology has two components. First, sociologists assume that their subject matter involves recurrent events. Second, they assume that describable relationships exist between selected aspects of these recurrent events. This is another way of saying that sociologists assume their subject matter to be determined. This is often accompanied by the belief that their subject matter is a closed system, i.e., that the only "good" sociological theory is one in which social facts are used to explain social facts. This, however, is not a necessary corollary and is usually waived by those sociologists whose methodological training has included material other than Durkheim's *The Rules of Sociological Method*.

A fourth, related assumption is that these relationships are sufficiently describable to permit the formulation of predictive and explanatory statements about sociology's subject matter. In other words, it is assumed not only that this subject matter is determined, but also that it is possible to formulate theoretical systems about it. This is not to assume any requirements for the form of such theories. Some sociologists see as desirable the formulation of universalistic, axiomatic theories, while others seek the formulation of statistical generalizations of limited applicability. But the condition is implicit that any sociological theories must predict and explain within tolerable margins of error. This, in turn, implies that the margins of error themselves are predictable and can be described and explained by any such theory.

The final assumption made by sociologists concerns the tolerability of the predictive margins of error. Sociologists assume that there can be indefinite improvement of the predictions and explanations of any sociological theory. Conversely, it is assumed that the margins of error tolerated in any sociological predicition can be indefinitely reduced through empirical research and systematic theorizing. In other words, sociologists assume their work to be progressive and cumulative, or at least potentially so.

The Core Theory Language of Sociology

Any theory is a special type of language system that can be analyzed into constituent parts. In the case of linguistic formulations, these parts are terms and statements. In the case of mathematical formulations, these parts are mathematical symbols and equations. Since sociological theory is so far primarily linguistic in volume, we shall be dealing with "terms" and "statements" in what follows. This analysis is equally applicable to mathematical formulations, however, as Chapter 4 will demonstrate.

The theory language of sociology consists of a core of central, substantive (or "extralogical") terms that are shared by the subdisciplines. It also consists of a body of peripheral terms that are peculiar to each subdiscipline. Thus, "status," "role," "social structure," "behavior patterns," "power," etc., are core terms; while demography employs such specialized terms as "viability," "birth rate," "death rate," "population shifts," etc.; social psychology such terms as "identity," "self," "anxiety level," "status inconsistency," etc.; social problems such terms as "deviance," "social control," "mental illness," "crime," etc.; and so on down the list of subdisciplines. Although we will deal primarily with the core terminology of sociology, this analysis applies equally to the peripheral, specialized terminologies.

The content of the statements in the sociological theory language varies widely across subdisciplines as well as within any one subdiscipline. This is also true of the substantive terms in these statements and of those terms that describe relationships ("logical" terms). However, the general *form* of these statements is constant throughout all of sociological theorizing: they are statistical generalizations. I shall postpone a detailed consideration of these types of statements until Chapters 2 and 3. Suffice it here to say that this commonality is a unifying attribute of sociology.

The Research Techniques of Sociology

Although the research techniques employed in sociology vary, they too have certain elements in common. One of the most important is the core theory language. Insofar as all sociological research techniques make use of this terminology, they share this attribute. It is possible to categorize all sociological research techniques on the basis of the relative use made of survey methods, experimental procedures, and observational technique, since none of these need be used to the exclusion of the others. This is not to rule out the possibility, of course, that any given piece of research will rely exclusively on one or another procedure. The clearest line of demarcation is between survey methods and experimental procedures (Cronbach, 1957). All require statistical analysis for evaluating their data.

The Fundamental Unit of Analysis of Sociology

There are many ways of identifying units of analysis in science. At one extreme, one can do it by edict; at the other, one can map correspondences between physical events and the terms used to designate these events. I shall choose the latter method to isolate the fundamental unit of analysis of sociology.

Human behavior is the core phenomenon about which all sociologists theorize. Attributes of it that interest them most are designated as "social." Although definitions of "social behavior" vary (Homans, 1961 and Weber, 1962a), fundamental to them is some concept of men's actions affecting the actions of other men. "Social behavior," then, is a relational term: it designates the various attributes of the relationships between actions of men and other actions of men. These attributes may

be temporal, situational, or descriptive of the topography of the particular behavior involved. The statement, "The teacher told the pupil to
read the book and he read it," designates a social act. It describes the
relationship between the teacher's behavior and pupil's. A detailed description of what the teacher said, how she said it, and what the child
did involves a description of the topographies of their behaviors. Temporal attributes include reference to when the behaviors occurred as
well as to certain temporal relations between the behaviors: e.g., how
soon did the pupil read the book after having been told to do so? Finally, situational attributes include such things as the physical setting
of the social act and the spatial arrangements of the actors.

Any attributes of human behavior that define it as social in this minimal sense are the central physical events of sociology. Any terms that
map direct correspondences to these events are the fundamental units
of analysis of sociology. That is, any terms that are used as if they
stood in a direct designative relationship with these events compose
these fundamental theoretical units. One thinks immediately of such
terms as "power," "social structure," "mutual expectations," "role,"
"status," "small group," "superordination-subordination," "influence,"
"authority," etc. These terms are then the fundamental units of analysis in sociology in two senses: first, they designate attributes of the only
physical events the sociologist can observe and in which he is inter-
ested, and second, they must be referred to in the definitions of any
terms the sociologist considers definable (as opposed to primitive
terms). These rather strong claims will be extensively justified in Chapter 3.

The Basic Argument of the Book

Given these parameters of sociology, I will evaluate it as a theory language system, using two basic criteria: its semantic worth and its logical worth. The first has to do with the meaning of its core terms. How
well delineated are the correspondences between physical events and
the terms that designate these events? What semantic problems are involved? Are sociological definitions fruitful? Are the terms used in the

way they would be used in a true theory language? The second has to do with the relations between the core terms and the other component terms of the statements in which they appear, as well as the relationships between the statements of sociological theory. Is sociological theory adequately codified and systematized? How are abstract terms best used in sociological theory? What is the basic status of such terms at present? Does sociology have an adequate theory language? Do the present strategies of sociological research provide investigative procedures that are sufficient to formulate a sociological theory language and to verify its worth after formulation? The two evaluative criteria obviously overlap, as will many of the critical issues to follow.

Chapter 1 will present some of the basic concepts needed to evaluate sociological theory language: referential meaning, grammar, contextual meaning, definition, and scientific vs. conventional language systems. Chapter 2 will discuss some basic language problems and their relevance for sociology: vagueness, ambiguity, opacity, and contradiction as these apply to meaning, definition, grammar, and context. The distinction between scientific and conventional language systems will be elaborated. It will be demonstrated that sociological language is more like a conventional than a scientific language system, both in terms of the above problems and in its failure to use adequate procedures to control those problems. Chapter 3 will reveal some of the most blatant problems in existent sociological theorizing and research, arising from the general problems discussed in Chapter 2. Special emphasis will be placed on the theoretical fruitfulness of sociological theory language and on the nature of sociological predictions, data, terminology, and research strategies. Chapter 4 will examine three solutions to these problems that have been proposed by sociologists: the explication of present sociological terminology, the codification of existent theories into mathematical models and axiomatic form, and the study of observable human behavior by ethnomethodologists and exchange theorists. The sufficiency of these solutions will be examined. Briefly, by way of conclusion, the parameters of a total solution to sociology's language problems will be delineated.

The primary orientation of this book is formal and logico-deductive rather than empirical or metaphysical. I will not address myself to questions about the ultimate reality with which sociologists should be concerned, but rather to the linguistic and logico-deductive forms most fruitful in dealing with the reality with which they are concerned. That is, I accept the legitimacy of the subject matter and make the assumptions required.

ONE

Basic Concepts

Limiting the Universe of Discourse: Nominals, Predicates, and Referential Meaning

ANY LANGUAGE can be described by the categories of linguistic elements that compose it. The exact categories used will depend upon the way in which the particular analyst has segmented the linguistic events he is concerned with, i.e., the particular units of analysis he is employing. This in turn will be determined by the purpose of his analysis. Thus, a grammarian deals with grammatical categories of linguistic elements such as nouns, verbs, adjectives, etc., as opposed to a psycholinguist who may study the effects of such types of statements as questions, instructions, or imperatives on nonlinguistic behavioral events. The philosophy of science also suggests which particular categories of linguistic elements an analyst should employ. I shall concentrate on words which fall into the categories of nominals and predicates. This will exclude any (but the most superficial) consideration of isolated articles, pronouns, and connective devices ("and," "or," "if . . . then," "if . . . and only if . . . ," "either . . . or . . . ," etc.). The former terms are called the extralogical terms of language. Nominals include nouns, verbs, and qualifiers such as adjectives, adverbs, and quantifiers (e.g., "more," "less," "ten," etc.). Predicates include any form of linguistic element that stands in an identity relationship to a nominal: for example, in the sentence "social status is X" the unspecified variable X is the predicative element. The verb "to be" is the most usual connective device in identity relations. In this capacity it is equivalent to the insertion of an " = " sign between the particular nominal and predicate: e.g., "social status is X" is the same as "social status $= X$". Since predicates are given a functional definition, the same categories of words (nouns, verbs, etc.) can be either nominals or predicates depending on how they are juxtaposed in a statement. In the sentence, "John is a boy," "John" is a nominal and the phrase "a boy" a predicate; if the sentence is transposed, the reverse is true: in the sentence "a boy is John," "a boy" is a nominal and "John" a predicate.

Of all the hypothesized types of meaning we will consider only the type most relevant for scientific language. This simplifies the discussion considerably, for it permits avoidance of the sticky debate as to the exact components of a word's meaning (compare, for example, Osgood et. al., 1957; Osgood, 1963; Morris, 1946; Brown, 1958; and Katz and Fodor, 1964). Scientific language must permit the manipulation of the observables that are the domain of any particular science. This can be accomplished only through the use of linguistic symbols that permit such manipulation. The linguistic symbols must at certain points represent observable attributes, properties, and relations. A term's referential meaning consists of the points of contiguity between it as linguistic symbol and the observable attributes, properties, and relations that it represents. Thus, referential meaning is the most relevant "meaning concept" for a consideration of scientific terminology.

If the above seems unclear it is because it presupposes a knowledge of some of what follows in this chapter.

Referential Meaning

BASIC DEFINITION

Terms and statements can be analyzed either functionally or formally (see Scriven, 1958). In the first case, terms and statements are treated as context-bound elements in a particular act of communication. In the second case, terms and statements are treated separately from their communicative context and analyzed as independent phenomena. The dimensions of this analysis will vary according to the purposes of the researcher: e.g., he may be a grammarian or a semanticist. This book will analyze formally the use of sociological terms and statements. Any given extralogical term or the statement in which it is embedded will be considered as a phenomenon separate from the communication act of which it is a part.

This general orientation has important consequences for the definition of referential meaning. If the analysis to follow were functional, referential meaning would have to be defined by reference to "stimuli," "responses," "messages," etc. In a formal analysis it can be defined by reference to simple and compound object predicates.

An object predicate is any extralogical term in predicative position that refers directly to observable objects, properties, or relations. These are observable inasmuch as two or more independent observers can certify their presence or absence in any given case. An object predicate, then, is a label affixed to particular, directly observable phenomena (see Hempel, 1952).

Object predicates may be simple or compound. Simple object predicates are either singular, unqualified extralogical terms or extralogical terms that are qualified by other extralogical terms. For example, in the identity statement, "High status is high income, education, and occupation," "high income, education, and occupation" is a simple object predicate consisting of three object predicates qualified by "high."

Compound object predicates are simple or compound clauses. For example, in the statement, "A person is said to have 'high status' if he tells another person to do something and then the other person complies," the "if . . . and then" fragment is a compound object predicate. Although the exact form of compound object predicates varies widely, the type most important for sociology is the conditional object predicate. A conditional object predicate is an object predicate that through logical connectives establishes empirical conditions under which the term can be said to apply. Logical connectives include "and," "or," "if . . . then," "if and only if," "either . . . or," and "neither . . . nor" embedded in statements. "If . . . then" is the logical connective most often used in conditional object predicates. In the above example, the "if . . . then" fragment is this type of conditional object predicate.

The referential meaning of any extralogical term is the ordered set of simple or compound object predicates that can be specified as capable of standing in an identity relation with that term. The member object predicates must be either specified or specifiable: they must have been previously used in this identity relation or must be capable of existing in this relation with the particular nominal. To return to the above examples, "high status" has been placed in identity relations with both "high income, education, and occupation" and person A telling person B to do something and person B complying. These two object predicates, then, are part of its specified referential meaning. Any future object predicates used in identity relations with "status" are potential components of its referential meaning. The members of the set can be ordered so that one particular object predicate can be said to be in an identity relation with the nominal across more contexts than the others. Conversely, one particular object predicate can be said to be in an identity relation with the nominal across fewer contexts than the others. In other words, the set of object predicates can be placed on a scale of "importance" from the most appropriate to the least in terms of the standing of each object predicate in an identity relation with the nominal. "Education, income, occupation" is a more important object predicate vis-à-vis "status" than "person A . . ." according to current usage in sociology. As shall be shown, this ordering is usually accomplished by explicit definition or by determining syntactical and contextual requirements. Moreover, the set which is the referential meaning of the term may have zero or one or more members and may be complete or incomplete, but it must have a finite number of members. Special cases of referential meaning in which the set has zero member predicates, is complete, or is unordered will be considered shortly.

CAN ABSTRACTIONS BE REFERENTIAL?

One might legitimately object that certain extralogical terms are apparently beyond such empirical accessibility. This class of terms is ordinarily called "abstractions" or "abstract entities." Can the meaning of such a term be referential? Can it be conceived of as ordered sets of object predicates? The answer is "yes" for two reasons. First, certain abstractions are composed of superordinate sets whose members consist of sets of lower-order abstractions, whose members, in turn, consist of ordered sets of object predicates. In fact, any extralogical term as an

ordered set of object predicates (even if there is only one member object predicate) is an abstraction, albeit a lower-order abstraction. Thus,
there is no extralogical term that is not an abstraction, although some
terms are higher or lower than others as abstractions. For example, the
term "social system" as an abstraction is usually defined by reference to
"the interrelationships between constituent elements." This predicate is
specifiable because the elements and the interrelationships can be defined. The requisite definitions to accomplish this will involve establishing identity relations between "interrelationships" and certain object predicates and between "elements" and certain object predicates:
e.g., "elements are people" and "the interrelationships are the issuance
of and compliance with commands or directives."

Second, other abstractions which are apparently devoid of referential
meaning are at some point in their context of usage specified or specifiable in terms of object predicates. In this case, compound object predicates and subordinate sets of object predicates will most likely form the
referential set of object predicates. This is equivalent to saying that any
extralogical term which is used and understood by a person conversant
in a particular language is definable by compound object predicates
merely by virtue of its use in extended statements. For example, "social
system" may be used in a sense in which it has no lower-order object
predicates. However, it will be specifiable by the use of compound
higher-order object predicates. Statements like the following are legitimate: " 'Social system' is that term which has been used in the following way by sociologists," the "that . . . which" clause being a compound object predicate.

CONNOTATIVE VS. DENOTATIVE REFERENTIAL MEANING

Whether complex or simple, the object predicates that are the
members of the set which comprises the referential meaning of a term
are specifiable. To be specifiable is quite different from having been
specified. The former refers to the *potential* for being specified, while
the latter refers to the *fact* of being specified. Two dimensions of
meaning are often distinguished on this basis: connotative or inten-
sional and denotative or extensional (see Berlo, 1960, and Lewis, 1952).
In its broadest sense, the referential denotative meaning of a term is
that subset of the set of simple or compound object predicates forming

the total meaning of the term whose members have been specified. The object predicate members of this subset are available and in common usage, and they would be listed as part of the particular term's meaning by people knowing the relevant language. For most sociologists, then, "socioeconomic status" and "authority relations" are part of the denotative meaning of "status." The referential connotative meaning of a term, on the other hand, consists of the subset of the set of object predicates forming the total meaning of a term whose members are specifiable but not immediately available or in common usage through knowledge of the language in question. Referential connotative meaning, then, is the potential referential meaning of a term. When people say they have an "intuitive understanding" or "gut feeling" as to the referential meaning of a term, they are giving evidence that they know a term's referential connotative meaning. They could specify the object predicates of the term's referential meaning after deliberation, given the consensus of other people who are familiar with the term's usage. For most sociologists, "status" means ranking people on certain social categories, but there is considerable variation among them as to the numbers and types of these categories. They are therefore part of the connotative referential meaning of "status."

Both of these dimensions co-vary. As the referential denotative meaning of a term is increased, its referential connotative meaning is decreased, and vice versa. In other words, as more of the specifiable object predicates of a term's total referential meaning becomes specified, there will be more specified object predicates. And conversely, as more of the specified object predicates of a term's referential meaning cease to be explicitly specified, there will be more potentially specifiable object predicates. Although at first the latter shift from specified to specifiable object predicates seems unlikely, with increased usage of a term it is quite possible. The familiar sociological distinction between "status" and "role" has become blurred with the extended application of the latter, and hence an increase in its connotative meaning.

CONTEXTUAL REFERENTIAL MEANING

Another important dimension of referential meaning has been called contextual meaning (Berlo, 1960). This refers to a shift in object predicates from one term to another due to the terms' association in an extended linguistic statement or context. If two (or more) terms are used contiguously in an extended linguistic statement (either verbal or textual) the probability is increased that the object predicates of one term will be associated with the object predicates of the other term(s). Depending on several factors, this association can result in the intersection of the sets, so that the referential meaning of both terms is comprised of some of the same object predicates. For example, consider the statement: "The family as an institution is losing its previous functions." Understanding of this statement requires some familiarity with the object predicates of "family" and "institution" and a transfer of some of the predicates from the latter to the former. This is necessary because one is considering the family "as" an institution. The problem with this concept is that the necessary and sufficient conditions that must hold for a linguistic statement if this intersection of sets is to occur have never been specified. It seems likely that such an intersection of sets would occur more often with an adjective qualifying a noun or with an adverb qualifying a verb than with other types of terms. But it is also possible that two nouns that have a contiguous relation in an extended linguistic statement would undergo an intersection of their sets of referential object predicates, as in the case of the above example.

Grammar

PRELIMINARIES TO A DEFINITION

It is necessary to distinguish between two main theoretical systems used to describe and define grammar. Lounsbury (1963) differentiates between the two systems on the basis of whether the rules used to generate a grammatical utterance are "formation rules" or "transformation rules." Bar-Hillel (1964) makes the same distinction. Chomsky (1965), also making the same distinction, calls the first type "structural grammar" and the second "generative grammar."

Structural grammar consists of rules for the generation of sentences word by word in terms of transitional dependencies. These transitional dependencies have been derived on the basis of past use of the words. "Categorical grammar," in which certain lexical items are categorized in given grammatical categories (e.g., "verbs," "nouns," etc.), and rules for the sequential ordering of members of these categories are provided, may be lumped in with this type.

There are two types of generative grammar. The first provides rules that permit the generation of all sentences of a language from a limited set of "kernel" sentences. The second supplies a basic "kernel" sentence, its possible expansions, and a set of transformational rules which specify certain conditional rearrangements of sentence elements.

Both systems have their champions as descriptive linguistic systems. Generally, more empirical research has been done on grammar as a sequential ordering of elements or classes of elements. Since (as shall be shown below) this formulation of grammar merges so well with the former section on meaning and conceptually solves some knotty linguistic problems, I shall select it arbitrarily as *the* appropriate model of grammar.

GRAMMAR AS WORD ORDER

Any sentence will have referentially meaningful extralogical terms that can best be described by sets of object predicates and by logical terms or other grammatical devices (like articles, conjunctions, etc.). The function of grammar is to order sequentially these extralogical sets of object predicates. This is done through the use of the logical terms as grammatical devices and also through a prior understanding and agreement by users of the language system that certain word orderings are "grammatically correct" or "grammatically understandable" and that other word orderings are not. Sequential ordering of the extralogical terms has the basic effect of assigning an order to the sets of object predicates involved. Or, to put it another way, the extralogical terms are sequentially ordered so as to increase the probability of the emission of certain object predicates and decrease the probability of the emission of other object predicates.

Consider the following sentence, for example: "Democracy is good if and only if 'good' means fair." The grammatical structure of this sentence includes its word order, the conjunction "and," and the logical connective "if and only if," which establishes an equivalence relation between "democracy" and "fair." These grammatical devices explicitly restrict the specifiable object predicates in the set "good" to the member object predicate "fair", and thereby permit the union of the set "good" and the set "democracy". Notice, also, that through this union of sets, "good" is given a higher probability of emission as a member of the set "democracy" than any other member of that set, providing that this sentence is taken as an isolated unit. What was done explicitly by way of illustration in this example occurs in every sentence or statement. Grammar allows people to understand a sentence by restricting the range of the object predicate members of the extralogical terms in the sentence, or, more correctly, by assigning specific probabilities of emission to the object predicate members of these terms. A greatest probability is usually assigned to one member predicate, assuring its priority over the rest. Special cases where this does not happen will be considered in the sections dealing with definition.

THE INTERDEPENDENCE BETWEEN GRAMMAR AND MEANING

Grammar and meaning (which is assumed for our purposes to be exclusively referential) are obviously not independent of one another. This formulation of grammar must make use of semantic information (knowledge of the sets of object predicates of the extralogical terms) as well as of transitional dependencies and sequential ordering. Katz and Fodor (1964) demonstrate the problems involved in trying to generate a given sentence according to semantic information alone; they find it difficult to avoid ambiguity and can manage to generate only a simple sentence that is four ways ambiguous. Chomsky (1965) and Cherry (1957: 112–20) amply demonstrate that reliance on transitional dependencies alone to generate a sentence can result in the formation of nonsense sentences and in the complete disregard of cases of semantic equivalence (or the union of the sets of two or more extralogical terms). Moreover, the interdependence of grammar and meaning is demonstrated by the fact that the total meaning of any logical connective or other grammatical device that is a single term (such as the conjunctions "and" and "but") can be formulated as a set of complex predicates that define the grammatical function of the term: e.g., " 'and' is that conjunction that is used to conjoin two clauses, phrases, etc.," where the "that is" clause is a complex object predicate. Scriven (1958) demonstrates this with the conjunction "but."

Grammar and contextual meaning are related concepts. An extralogical term acquires both grammatical and contextual meaning through its position in a linguistic statement. Thus, both types of meaning are derived from the relations between extralogical terms and logical terms as well as from other grammatical devices in statements of sentence, clause, or even phrase length or in statements that contain more than one sentence and, by implication, in multiple clauses and phrases. Moreover, the acquisition of both types of meaning depends on the repetition of these relations between extralogical terms and logical terms and the other grammatical devices in singular or multiple statements. For example, "dog" is taken to be a noun (a grammatical category) because of its repetitive use in noun-like position: it is qualified by an article, it often stands as the subject of a sentence(s) or clause(s), etc. Similarly, the set of object predicates of "dog" is altered by the repetitive relations it bears to other extralogical terms which stand in a qualifying relation to it: e.g. "The good dog. . . ." etc. Notice also that the adjective "good" acquires its function as an adjective (another grammatical category) by the repetition over singular and multiple statements of just this qualifying position in relation to nouns.

Given these points of similarity between contextual and grammatical meaning, it is important to note that they differ markedly in their respective ideal functions. Grammatical meaning refers to the restriction of possible object predicates of an extralogical term's referential meaning to (ideally) one object predicate. This is accomplished by the sequential ordering and by the transitional probabilities assigned to sentence elements or sets of sentences which, in turn, order the set of predicates. Contextual meaning refers to the intersection and in some special cases to the union of sets of object predicates of extralogical terms by virtue of their relative positions in singular or multiple, repetitive or unrepetitive statements. The ideal result of the union or intersection is the accumulation (or sharing) of object predicates by the terms, as opposed to the ideal grammatical function of restricting the available object predicates. In both cases, however, I am speaking of the "ideal" function of both types. As shall be shown below, this ideal is defined in terms of the objectives of conventional vs. scientific language use. It is frequently violated, however. The object predicates of extralogical terms are often assigned equal weight or go unspecified by virtue of the grammatical meanings of the terms in statements. And the object predicates of two or more extralogical terms can be logically inconsistent or in contradictory relations by virtue of their contextual meanings.

Definition

THE SPECIFICATION OF MEANING

Generally, any definition involves the specification and selection of a subset of object predicates from the total specifiable object predicates forming an extralogical term's meaning. The function of definition, then, is to convert specifiable object predicates into specified object predicates, or to increase the range of a term's denotative meaning and thereby decrease the range of its connotative meaning. Moreover, if a definition specifies more than one member object predicate, it should (ideally) assign a definite order to the predicates. The assignment of a definite order is usually accomplished by specifying the conditions under which any given object predicate in a set can be understandably used as the definition of a particular nominal. This order is determined by the ways in which the nominal may be used, given the differences between its meanings. For example, "power" refers to relationships between individuals and between collectivities. In certain contexts it may be used understandably only as it refers to individuals, while in others only as it refers to collectivities. It is the job of any definition of "power" to specify the object predicates associated with "power" and to order the object predicates by specifying the conditions under which each one may be used as the definition of "power." This ordering translates into a list of contexts in which "power" may be used to refer to individual or to collectivities.

RULES OF INCLUSION AND EXCLUSION

Definitions vary specifically along certain dimensions. First, all definitions employ either the principle of enumeration or rules of inclusion or exclusion in order to specify the defining object predicate members of a nominal's referential meaning. The principle of enumeration involves listing all relevant members. This can be accomplished by denoting the appropriate object predicates (pointing out their physical object counterparts), by ostensive definition (definition by example), by nominal definition (agreeing that certain object predicates should belong to the set of a given term), by real definition (the specification of the exclusive object predicates that *empirically* belong to the set of a given term), and by any form of conditional definition (see below). The principle of enumeration can also refer to the listing of those object predicates that do *not* belong to the defining subset of a term's referential meaning. This may be called negative definition (e.g., "a dog is not a cat, not a horse, not a whale, etc.") and is related to definition by rules of exclusion. Finally, definition by enumeration can employ positive as well as negative enumeration: e.g., "a dog is an animal, is furry, *and* is not a cat, not a horse, etc."

The rules of inclusion or exclusion state a criterion (or criteria) or a rule(s) for determining whether certain member predicates do or do not belong in the definitional subset. For example, a definition of "status" by a rule of inclusion would be: "Status is an individual's rank according to relative amount of income." One need not enumerate the ranks of all individuals according to amount of income because the rule of inclusion is sufficient to classify any individual's status, given information on his income. A definition of "status" by a rule of exclusion would be: "Status is *not* how a particular person performs when given a task." One is narrowing down the range of referential meaning of the term by saying what "status" is not. Obviously, before rules of exclusion can fully define a term they must delimit those object predicates that are part of a term's meaning, and this requires delimiting all those object predicates that are not part of the meaning of the term. (Because this is impossible, they usually function as supplements to rules of inclusion: "Status is not how a person performs when given a task, but is rather his sanctioned duty in performing a task.")

CONDITIONAL VS. UNCONDITIONAL DEFINITIONS

It should be clear by now that definitions vary according to whether the object predicates they specify are conditional and/or unconditional. Definitions can be said to vary according to the relative amount and importance of each type of predicate used therein. Therefore, the dimension of conditional vs. unconditional predicates is actually a continuum.

Operational definitions (see Bridgeman, 1927) and reduction sentences (see Carnap, 1953) are almost purely conditional definitions. For example, Hempel (1952: 25–28) defines the simplest type of reduction sentence, which is sufficient to illustrate the above point.

$P_1X\ (QX = P_2X)$ can be translated:

"If an object X has characteristic P_1 (e.g., X is subjected to specified test conditions or to some specified stimulus) then the attribute Q is to be assigned to X if and only if X shows the characteristic (i.e., the reaction, the mode of response) P_2."

Where P_1 is produced by an observer at will, this reduction sentence is an operational definition (see Carnap, 1953). Nominal definitions, ostensive definitions, and real definitions can be pure unconditional definitions: e.g., "a dog is a furry animal" (a real definition). Any type of definition can be both conditional and unconditional, as is the case with the above definition of status. "Person A" and "person B" are specifiable by unconditional predicates, whereas "to do something" must be specified by conditional predicates employing spatio-temporal referents as conditions: "to do something is to start running at point Z at time$_1$ and stop running at point W at time$_2$." In fact, most definitions contain both conditional and unconditional predicates and therefore are not strictly one or the other type.

Definitional chains of both conditional and unconditional predicates complicate this mixture of types even further. Using the above example again, notice that a conditional definition of "to do something" would actually involve multiple conditional definitions in order to completely specify the "something." For example, "to do something" could be specified as "to run," "to walk," "to talk," and these, in turn, would necessitate conditional definitions specifying such object predicates as the relevant spatio-temporal referents and the actual behaviors involved in the activity. Given the above definition of "status," also notice that multiple unconditional object predicates could be specified for "tells," depending on the linguistic unit of analysis one is employing, thereby permitting the use of multiple unconditional definitions in its specification; e.g., "to tell" may be to utter "a word," "a sentence," "a paragraph," etc. Chains of operational definitions or reduction sentences would contain more conditional definitions than unconditional ones, while nominal, real, and ostensive definitional chains are more often (though not necessarily) weighted with unconditional object predicates.

THE EMPIRICAL ACCESSIBILITY OF SETS OF OBJECT PREDICATES

Definitions can vary according to the relative empirical accessibility of the sets of object predicates they specify. Abstract object predicates (conditional and unconditional) as superordinate sets of object predicates (conditional and unconditional) whose members are actually subsets of object predicates whose members, in turn, are subsets of these subsets of object predicates, and so on, are further removed from empirical accessibility than object predicates that refer directly to observables. There are primitive theoretical terms in theoretical language systems that are not defined explicitly through the specification of empirically accessible object predicates or even abstract object predicates. These are of two kinds. The first kind is made up of abstract terms that are implicitly defined by contextual and grammatical context within a theoretical system; "temperature" is an example in thermodynamics (Scriven, 1958). The second kind consists of object predicates that are taken to represent, directly and inclusively, physical objects, properties, or relations; "particle" is an example in physics. Between these two kinds lie the derived terms (see Margenau, 1950) that are specified by conditional and/or unconditional definitions and definitional chains of varying complexity; "social system" is an example in sociology. The first kind of primitive term is the lowest in empirical accessibility; the second kind of primitive term is the highest in empirical accessibility; and derived terms lie all the way along the continuum between these extreme cases.

Conventional vs. Scientific Linguistic Usage

A distinction between scientific and conventional language usage can be made on the basis of these concepts. The next chapter will discuss this distinction in detail. For the present, it will suffice to specify its basic parameters. Scientific language systems demand greater explicit control of language usage than conventional language systems. By explicit control over language usage is meant the degree to which the users of a language employ devices to increase the precision of their usage. Precision of usage of any linguistic element refers to the extent to which users agree on the correct or appropriate usage of that linguistic element, be it a word or a complete sentence (see Naess, 1952).

Agreement between users of linguistic elements has three components: semantic agreement, grammatical agreement, and contextual agreement. Given the above emphasis on referential meaning, semantic agreement has to do with the degree to which an extralogical term's defining referential predicates are assessed to be both necessary and sufficient for the application of the term to empirical situations. This assessment must involve a consensus among the users of the given term. In other words, semantic agreement refers to a judgment by the users of a term that the term's object predicates reliably reflect the empirical reality they are supposed to reflect. Grammatical agreement refers to the interuser evaluation that given linguistic statements are grammatically correct. Since, as was shown earlier in this chapter, referential meaning and grammar are interdependent, it follows that semantic agreement and grammatical agreement are interdependent. This is not to say that one implies the other, however. There can be grammatical agreement about a linguistic statement that has few meaningful terms. Epstein (1961) demonstrated this by using sentences composed of nonsense syllables. Conversely, there can be agreement about the meaningfulness of component words in an ungrammatical or even grammatically nonsensical statement. Contextual agreement refers to the interuser agreement on just how the object predicates of one extralogical term are affected by the object predicates of another extralogical term. Do the sets intersect? Is there a union of sets? What members are transposed? When questions such as these are answered through an understanding among users, contextual agreement pertains.

Devices That Increase Precision of Usage

DEFINITION

Any device to increase the precision of language usage must deal with all the above components of interuser agreement. The explicit definition of terms is the most common device employed to achieve semantic agreement. But, as we have seen, this device can also be used to define a logical or extralogical term's grammatical meaning by specifying conditional object predicates that refer to the term's relative position and linguistic function in a given linguistic statement. Therefore, definition can be used as a device to increase grammatical as well as semantic agreement. Furthermore, definitional chains may suffice to increase contextual agreement. The simplest such chain would involve a definition of the extralogical term one is concerned with and then a second definition redefining this term. The redefinition would consist of simple object predicates and of conditional object predicates that relate the particular extralogical term to the other term (or terms) that give it a particular contextual meaning. By way of example consider the following such chain:

Definition 1: "A dog is a furry animal."
Definition 2: "A dog is a good, furry animal, if the word 'dog' is embedded in context X (X may be further specified through the use of conditional object predicates)."

SYSTEMATIZATION

Semantic, grammatical, and contextual agreement may be increased by a process I shall call "systematization." This involves the ordering of linguistic elements and the specifying of the exact relations between them so that the deductive and inductive logical processes are facilitated.

The types of systematization vary according to their degrees of sophistication. The level of precision of language usage usually varies with the degrees of sophistication of the types of systematization. At one extreme, a rambling set of statements can be systematized so that qualifiers are directly associated with what they qualify, nominals are placed in nominal position, predicates are placed in predicative position and are juxtaposed to the appropriate nominals, and so on. At this level, any time a person reroutes or rephrases a given statement or set of statements he is attempting to systematize them. The essential linguistic elements are not altered, but their relative positions and relations are modified to make the statement clearer. At the other extreme, are axiomatization and the use of mathematical models. Axiomatization involves the ordering of limited sets of statements from the general to the specific, thereby creating a deductive hierarchy, in which one statement can be derived from another and the logical relations between statements can be specified. Mathematical model building involves the translation of linguistic expressions into mathematical symbols and formulae. Both of these will be discussed extensively in Chapter 4.

Any type of systematization is generally used to increase language precision through the reduction of grammatical and contextual ambiguities and inconsistencies. This, in turn, increases the levels of contextual and grammatical agreement or usage. However, systematization may indirectly affect semantic agreement through its effects on context and grammar, given the interdependencies between these three entities.

The Restriction of Empirical Utility

Scientific language usage labors under the restriction of empirical utility, whereas this is not necessarily true of conventional usage. Scientific language must permit the prediction and control or, at least, the prediction of empirical events. Conventional language can afford the luxury of polite conversation and chitchat (as well as serious conversation) that has no actual or intended effect on empirical events. The restriction of empirical utility necessitates a high degree of precision in scientific language, and therefore a high degree of explicit language control to increase the degree of interuser semantic, grammatical, and contextual agreement. This, in turn, necessitates the extensive use of definition and systematization. Conventional language also employs these control devices, but less extensively and less explicitly than scientific language. It employs them in accordance with the whims of circumstance and the vagaries of labile exigencies. Scientific language employs them consistently, determinately, and with steadfastness of purpose. It is in this respect that scientific and conventional language usage differ most sharply.

The Metalanguage of Logic

Another way of putting all this is that scientific language employs a metalanguage to control itself. This metalanguage is logic. The devices of control used to increase precision are explicit definition and logical systematization; the metalanguage treats scientific language as a closed system. Conventional language employs no such systematic metalanguage in its own control. True, it uses some of the same devices as scientific language to increase its precision, but these devices are employed in psycholinguistic contexts and are therefore subject to varying contingencies. Conventional language is not controlled from above or outside the psycholinguistic context by a universalistic language system. The devices of control are generated from within the varying psycholinguistic situations and employed to remedy specific instances of imprecision. The controlling metalanguage of scientific language, on the other hand, states universalistic rules of usage that are specifically applicable to many cases of a given type and generally applicable to cases of all types.

These distinctions between scientific language usage and conventional language usage will assume great importance when we consider the problems of sociological language use.

A Word of Caution

Linguists and philosophers of science could take exception to some of the statements made in this chapter. Let me caution the sociologist, then, to use these basic concepts as sensitizing concepts. They are heuristic devices which will be used in subsequent chapters to handle certain sociological issues.

They will not be used to buttress false arguments, but rather to point out and clarify certain problems.

Before turning to Chapter 2, I must call attention to two rather oversimplified statements made for heuristic purposes in this chapter. First of all, I purposely overextended the application of the term "object predicate" to cover conditional and abstract predicates. The only basis on which this extension could be justified is the fact that conditional and abstract predicates can be translated into object predicates. Not only can the degree of justification thereby attained be questioned, but so can the translation itself (see the section on "The Observability of Referents of Terms" in the next chapter). Second, the distinction drawn in the preceding section between scientific language usage and conventional language usage is not hard and fast. As Scriven (1958) has noted, any analysis of scientific language usage must take into consideration functional (psycholinguistic) relationships in the use of language. Hempel (1958: 53) implicitly acknowledges this also in his formal requirement that before a given term can be used in a (scientific) theory language, a set U of conventional sentences in which the term has been appropriately used must be specified; and U must be necessary and sufficient for the term to be understood prior to its introduction into the (scientific) theory language. Moreover, Naess (1952 and 1953) presents an intriguing formulation of one aspect of verbal interaction as the progressive definition and redefinition of imprecise terms (the conventional language realm) to levels of increasing precision and agreement (the scientific language realm). Therefore, the above distinction breaks down in two directions: conventional language must be employed to formulate scientific language, and scientific language can be used to describe processes in conventional language.

These admitted transgressions nevertheless preserve the proper substance of certain key concepts and will prove valuable in the following chapters. They do not destroy my basic argument.

Summary

All words can be categorized initially as "nominals" or "predicates" according to their juxtaposition in statements. Any term's referential meaning is the set or subset of object predicates that stand in an identity relation with the term. Object predicates can be single words, words qualifying other words, or phrases and clauses that determine the conditions under which the identity relation applies. Abstract terms can be analyzed in this manner because they are either sets whose subsets are terms whose subsets are, in turn, object predicates or they are specifiable at some point in their context of usage as sets of conditional object predicates. The connotative referential meaning of a term consists of those sets or subsets of object predicates that are specifiable: they can be specified in the future but are not specified in the present. The denotative referential meaning of a term consists of those sets or subsets of object predicates that are specified: the user of the term can list them upon request. Contextual referential meaning refers to any operations occurring to these sets or subsets because of their juxtaposition in extended linguistic statements.

Grammar is defined as the sequential ordering of terms in statements. It is interdependent with meaning in the sense that it acts as an ordering device for the member predicates of the sets and subsets of sequentially ordered terms. It is interdependent with contextual meaning because this ordering effect selects those object predicates that combine in specific ways through the contextual juxtaposition of two or more terms. It is different from contextual meaning because it tends to restrict the range of object predicates of a term, whereas contextual meaning tends to increase this range or alter it in ways other than restriction.

Definition involves the selection and ordering of the set of object predicates of a term. It converts connotative meaning into denotative meaning: the specifiable is specified. It varies along certain dimensions according to the rules of transformation applied to these sets of object predicates. It can select object predicates by rules of inclusion or exclusion; it can emphasize conditional object predicates, it can impose restrictions as to the degree of empirical accessibility of the object predicates, and finally, it can posit the presumed completeness or incompleteness of the selected object predicates.

A distinction can be made between conventional and scientific language systems, based on these linguistic concepts. Scientific language systems demand higher levels of precision of language usage than do conventional language systems. Precision of usage refers to the level of agreement as to usage among members of a language community. This has three components. Semantic agreement refers to the judgment by the users of a term that the term's object predicates reliably designate the empirical reality they are supposed to designate. Grammatical agreement refers to interuser evaluations that given linguistic statements are grammatically correct. Contextual agreement refers to interuser agreement on just how the object predicates of one term are affected by the object predicates of another term. Scientific language systems employ two basic devices to maintain high levels of precision of usage: definition and systematization. The latter refers to an appeal to the requirements of logic, as well as to the parsimony, organizational elegance, and simplicity enforced by scientific language systems. In a sense, these control devices function as a metalanguage governing scientific language systems. No such metalanguage exists for conventional language.

[TWO]

Problems with Sociological Language

GIVEN THE preceding formal analysis of language, it is possible to specify some linguistic problems that are extremely important for sociological theory. Sociology's basic weakness has to do with its theory language. Sociological theory language is more like conventional than like scientific language.

Vagueness

A term is said to be vague when the range of object predicates forming a term's referential meaning has not been specified: the term's connotative meaning is greater than its denotative meaning. In extreme cases, a vague term may have multiple, equiprobable, *specifiable* object predicates and no specified object predicates. The term "fucking" (in the vernacular) is often used so excessively in any (slang) linguistic statement that it has become vague in the extreme sense. All extralogical terms, however (even scientific ones that are precisely used), have varying degrees of vagueness.

The vagueness of sociological terms is well documented and widely accepted (see, for example, Blumer, 1954; Scriven, 1956b; Bergman, 1956). By way of example, consider the following statement from one of Weber's classic essays (Weber, 1962b: 181): "The way in which so-

cial honor is distributed in a community between typical groups par-
ticipating in this distribution we may call the 'social order.' " What
classes of object predicates, designating what classes of observable
events, are to be included in the referential meaning of "community"?
These are not specified. With some effort on the part of the reader,
certain of these classes could be isolated. However, it is important to
note that they are not initially specified: hence the vagueness of this
term. The same is true of "social honor," "typical groups," and the
phrase, "The way in which social honor is distributed."

Consider another example: "It [sociology] seeks to explain the nature of social order and social disorder." "Social order" is then contex-
tually modified by such terms and phrases as "events occur in a more-
or-less regular sequence or pattern," "individual life," "collective life,"
"balance of forces," etc. (Inkeles, 1964: 24). Neither the nominal "social order" nor any of its qualifying phrases or terms include references
to specified object predicates. Nor is it possible to argue that their referential meanings are well enough known to obviate this necessity.
These terms are equally vague.

Both the vagueness of a term and its range of connotative meaning
are defined by the number of specifiable object predicates in that
term's referential meaning. It follows that terms that are very vague
have, by definition, high levels of connotative meaning. Sociological
terms, then, are high in connotative meaning. The now-famous debate
over the implications of the structural-functional perspective of society
is an excellent example of this in sociology (see Merton, 1957:
37–45). Briefly, this perspective seemed to imply that the status quo
was the "ideal good," and, conversely, that change and conflict were
"bad". Much of the confusion stemmed from the equivalence in connotative meaning between the terminology used by the "structural-
functionalists" and conventional terminology. To say that every "social structure has a function" was taken to be equivalent to saying "the
established ways of doing things serve a purpose which justifies their
continuance." This equivalence was legitimately derivable because the
range of referential meaning of "social structure" and "function" was
never established. It did seem that part of the connotative meaning of
"function" was "implicit legitimacy." And "social structure" was applied to any and all instances of social organization. The entire debate

about this issue in sociology can therefore be viewed as an attempt to restrict the connotative meaning of the relevant terms.

Ambiguity

Any term is ambiguous when more than two but a finite number of object predicates have been specified as equiprobable members of the set comprising its referential meaning. The crux of the issue lies in the word "equiprobable." A less precise way of saying the same thing is that any term is ambiguous if it has multiple, equally legitimate meanings.

Sociological terms are highly ambiguous. Every time a researcher reviews the literature in order to derive the meanings of particular terms, he proclaims the ambiguity of these terms. This has been done with such terms as "status," "power," "role," and "status inconsistency." Although Kroeber and Kluckhohn's (1952) specification of the multiple meanings of "culture" is claimed to be an anthropological endeavor, it is also an excellent illustration of ambiguity in a core term used in sociology. Conversely, every time a researcher defines a core term differently from the way it has previously been defined, he is increasing the ambiguity of that term. Given the general laxity of sociological language usage, most researchers are guilty of this at one time or another.

More specifically, consider the following example: "I assume that the proper study of interaction is not the individual and his psychology, but rather the syntactical relations among the acts of different persons mutually present to one another" (Goffman, 1967:2).

Linguists have precise alternative meanings for syntax or grammar: there are transformational grammars, categorical grammars, phrase-structure grammars, and transitional grammars. Moreover, there are other particularistic grammars whose rules are precisely specified. Goffman does not specify which type of syntax or grammar he is referring to in the above phrase. This makes the phrase at least four ways ambiguous, for each type of grammar can be specified as a member of the set of object predicates that is the total referential meaning of "syntactical relations."

("Acts" is a vague term as used in Goffman's statement. In this respect it is accordingly analyzable. Furthermore, "psychology" is another example of a vague term. It has multiple, equiprobable, specifiable object predicates. The class of attributes that may characterize an individual *as* his "psychology" is quite extensive, and if this term is equivalent to "the behaviors of the individual," which it can be, this class of attributes is infinite.)

Opacity

Opacity refers to the failure of a term's reference function because there is no referent object of the sort represented by the term's object predicates (Quine, 1960: 151). Given my extension of the use of "object predicate" to cover all predicative instances, the precise application of "opacity" becomes problematic. Even such terms as "Satan" and "unicorn," which are used as traditional examples of opacity, can be designated by conditional object predicates (in this broadest sense): " 'Satan' is that term which is used in the following sense . . ." The following amended definition will suffice to circumvent this problem: Only those object predicates that designate, or are assumed to designate, properties, objects, or relations of empirical reality will be said to be opaque if, in fact, they do not so designate properties, objects, or relations of empirical reality. This problem is analogous to that of "reification," which should be familiar to most sociologists. Beck's (1953) analysis of "inferred entities" is also relevant.

Opacity is most often a question of the improper use of a term. It is quite unusual to confuse the validity of the reference function of a term. It is quite common, on the other hand, to use legitimate terms in an opaque fashion. This occurs when a term that should be defined is used without being or having been defined. In other words, a term is used opaquely if it is used as if it designated directly observable objects, properties, or relations when, in fact, it does not and cannot without prior definition.

This problem is particularly prevalent in sociology. Words like "status," "role," "institution," "organization," "social structure," "society," "norm," "power," "authority," "class," etc., are continually used as if they designated directly observable things: i.e., they are used in this manner when they must be defined in order to designate these things. For example, Zetterberg (1965: Chapter 1) notes that the data of sociology should be "actors and their actions." He then posits "types of actions" as though these were the empirical realities, "the actions of actors," that sociologists should study. "Types of actions," as he uses the phrase, are not empirical realities but inferential realities based on the observation of empirical realities. Similarly, Inkeles frequently uses the terms "social act" and "social order" to explicate the concerns of sociology (1964: 25–27). These terms do not refer directly to empirical events. Hence they are opaque. And sociologists generally use the phase "the role of" to qualify certain terms that designate certain people: e.g., "the role of the patient," "the role of the sick," "the role of the doctor" (Bloom, 1963). There is no such entity as a "role." The term does not and cannot without previous definition designate discriminable empirical events. Used in the above and similar contexts, it is opaque.

A final excellent example of this problem is Parsons' *The Social System* (1951). The term "social system" is used opaquely throughout. According to logical convention, when one refers to terms, the terms should be in quotation marks. When one uses terms to refer to things, then no quotation marks are needed. This practice is meant to avoid confusing the term with the thing that it is supposed to designate: i.e., to avoid opacity (see Quine, 1951: 23–33). Even the title of Parsons' book should therefore be *The "Social System"*. This term cannot be used as if it were a primitive term standing in one-to-one correspondence with empirical events. If it is to be analyzed as a thing, it must be analyzed as a term, not an empirical event, and therefore must be in quotation marks (see Lachenmeyer, 1970 for such an analysis).

Contradiction

Contradiction is a special case of ambiguity that occurs when a term has two different, equiprobable object predicates specified as its referential meaning and these object predicates are logically inconsistent. In this case, the predicates cannot both stand in identity relation with the nominal, since they both cannot be equivalent to the nominal. The

most common form of contradiction is the assertion that a thing is both
something and not something, one being the converse of the other:
e.g., "the ball is round and not round" or "the ball is round and
square."

This problem is pertinent for sociology in two ways. First, it occurs
frequently in sociological theorizing, depending upon the logical rigor
of the theorist. For example, Homans declares (1961: 34) that what he
calls "sentiments" are, in fact, "activities." On the same page, he asserts
that "sentiments resemble other activities." Again on the same page is
found this statement: "Among the many sentiments we shall be particularly concerned with social approval." Implicit in these latter two
statements is the notion that "sentiments" are somehow different from
"activities." "Social approval," then, is a sentiment. As such, it is both
the same as an activity and different from an activity. The contradiction is obvious. Everytime he uses the word "sentiment" in the subsequent text, it is semantically contradictory. Or consider the following
statement by Blau (1964: xxiii):

> The very processes that restore social equilibrium are usually disequilibra-
> ting forces in other respects. Since social forces may have contradictory
> implications, and since rigidities may require opposition forces to gather
> momentum before they can effect adjustment, structural change tends to
> assume a dialectical pattern of intermittent reorganizations.

This statement summarizes Blau's dialectical argument about the necessary occurrence of social change. He emphasizes the inherent contradiction in the empirical events involved. I would like to suggest that
this contradiction is an attribute of his theory rather than the phenomena with which he is concerned. "Event A may occur and its opposite
event B may also occur" is the requisite rewriting of his statement that
would clarify this point. This can be true or false, but it is not necessarily true or false as it stands. That is, insufficient information is con-
veyed to make it empirically confirmable. Are we to confirm A's occurrence before or after B's or vice versa? Are we to confirm A's
occurrence in spatial proximity with B or vice versa? Moreover, definite spatio-temporal values must be supplied, whichever is the case.

If Blau means this statement as a general theoretical proposition, it is
clearly contradictory because it leads to the deduction of logically inconsistent general statements. Consider the following deduced interpre-

tation, for example: "If process A is socially equilibratory, it will be socially equilibratory and socially disequilibratory." This contradiction, then, is inherent in his theory.

The second way contradiction manifests itself in sociology involves one of the basic assumptions of the discipline and, therefore, is not as easily corrected as is simple lack of logical rigor. This has to do with the "*sui generis* fallacy." Durkheim (1958) first burdened sociology with the aura of mysticism surrounding social facts as phenomena *sui generis*. By this he meant (as any sociologist knows) that the phenomena sociology is to deal with are composed of individual actors and their individual actions but are somehow more than these individual actors and their individual actions. Thus social institutions and organizations are composed of individual actors and actions, but they are wholes in and of themselves, which extend beyond individual actors and actions and therefore warrant a separate field of study. How can the whole be both the sum of its parts and more than the sum of its parts? Empirically, it cannot be. The "*sui generis* fallacy" is just that because it places empirical events on an equivalence basis with perceptual and inferential events. Individual actors and their actions are observable, empirical events. When these actors and their actions are summated and then described in terms that purport to refer to more than the summation, one is dealing with inferred entities, labels, abstractions, etc., that are derived from these empirical events but are not observable empirical events in and of themselves. But both the empirical events and the inferences based on these events are given equivalent status as empirical events and, furthermore, are assigned equivalent weight as object predicates standing in an identity relation with the particular nominal (be it "group," "institution," "organization," "society," etc.). Since the "*sui generis* fallacy" places two such logically inconsistent object predicates in an identity relation with the particular nominal, it is a prime example of contradiction in sociological terminology.

Problems of Grammar: Ambiguity, Vagueness, Contradiction, and Opacity

Since grammar and referential meaning are not independent, it is logical that the above forms of linguistic problems will have their grammatical representatives. The grammar of a sentence can fail to function adequately, thereby resulting in ambiguity, vagueness, contradiction, or even opacity in the component extralogical terms. This situation can be distinguished from ambiguity, vagueness, and contradiction in the grammatical devices per se. Obviously, this distinction is one of degree rather than kind.

When the grammar of a sentence fails to restrict the number of object predicates of the component extralogical terms, so that the multiple predicates (more than two, but a finite number) are specified and equiprobable, that grammar is ambiguous. When the multiple object predicates are specifiable rather than specified that grammar is vague. In this case, the grammar is intact and appropriate but insufficient to restrict the ambiguity and vagueness of the component extralogical terms.

Grammatical ambiguity and vagueness may also refer to ambiguity and vagueness in certain categories of grammatical word types. As we have seen, these categories of words are defined according to certain relationships their members bear to members of other categories. Thus, pronouns are defined according to the degree to which they can be substituted for nouns or, in some cases, noun phrases. Ambiguity and vagueness in pronominal reference are common examples of this type of grammatical ambiguity and vagueness. Miller (1962) gives the example, "they are eating apples," which can be analyzed as a case of pronominal reference in which "they" can refer to the noun phrase "eating apples" or can refer to some unspecified but specifiable group or groups of persons. Quine (1960) lists another form of vagueness occurring when there is cross reference to indefinite antecedents, as in the sentence: "Everything has a part smaller than it." Wender (1967) also presents another good example of vagueness: "Nonquantifying quantifiers (sort of, kind of, more or less, somewhat)." Ullman (1962) and

Quine speak of ambiguity in terms of grouping, another possible form under this type. Quine's example is the phrase "pretty little girls' camp," which can have four possible readings depending how one groups the components, e.g., pretty little, girls' camp, etc. Quine also speaks of ambiguity of scope, which I would term vagueness. His example is, "big European butterflies." Is this statement true of just European butterflies that are big compared to other European ones or the European butterflies that are big compared to any butterflies? Quine suggests another form of ambiguity which occurs when there is indeterminacy between the position of adjectives: e.g., "poor violinist" can have two or more possible readings. (This example obviously borders on what I call "contradiction.")

In the same vein, the grammar of a sentence can be contradictory by failing to restrict contradictory extralogical terms or by being contradictory in and of itself, that is, by utilizing contradictory grammatical devices. Katz's (1964b) systematic and exhaustive treatment provides many examples of the first type of grammatical contradiction. In a contradictory "copula sentence" an antonymous predicate is placed in an identity relation with a nominal: "the round table is square." A transformationally compound sentence is contradictory if the matrix sentence and the sentence embedded in the matrix to form the sentence are inconsistent. For example, a contradictory relative clause can be embedded in a matrix sentence to form a contradictory "transformationally compound sentence": "The ball which is round and square is black." Logical connectives can also be used in a way to permit (and to promote) contradiction in the extralogical terms of a sentence. Consider the following examples:

Negation: "something is something and *not* that something."
Conjunction: "something is something *and* something else," when both are mutually exclusive.
Disjunction: "something is that *or* this," when it is actually both.
Implication: "*if* something *then* something" which is its opposite.
Equivalence: "*if and only if* something *then* something else" which is its opposite.

Contradiction in grammatical devices per se is a special case of ambiguity and vagueness in grammatical devices per se in that with grammatical contradiction (of this type) the object predicates of the grammatical devices are specified as two in number, are equiprobable, and are logically inconsistent. Thus, any of the examples used above in relation to the second type of grammatical ambiguity and vagueness would suffice here, provided these conditions are satisfied.

GRAMMATICAL OPACITY: SYSTEMATICALLY MISLEADING EXPRESSIONS

It is difficult to specify opacity in grammatical devices as a type of grammatical opacity, but the grammar of a sentence can function to permit opacity in one or more of the component extralogical terms. Gilbert Ryle (1960) refers to such instances as "systematically misleading expressions." Such expressions are characterized by grammatical structures that give the component extralogical terms the appearance of denoting empirical referents when in actuality they do not.

To oversimplify his presentation, there are two basic types of these expressions. In the first, a compound predicative expression is designated by a more abstract term, and this term is used as a nominal. Hence, the term is used as a nominal when it is actually a predicative expression. One of his examples is "Virtue is its own reward," which should read, "Those who are virtuous . . ." Without the latter interpretation, the term "virtue" appears to directly designate observable entities. In the second type, "the" stands before a term so that the term appears to designate a thing when in actuality it does not. For example, consider this statement: "The middle of the tree has dense foliage." There is no empirical entity, "the middle of the tree." This phrase seems to refer to a thing, but in actuality it refers to a relative positioning among many things. The "the" therefore inappropriately lends legitimate status to an opaque term. The types of expressions are related in that "the" phrases can be predicative expressions disguised as nominals, as in the above example. That is, the second type of systematically misleading expressions can also be the first type. However, this need not be the case, as in the following example of Ryle's: "Poincaré is not the King of France," when there is no King of France.

GRAMMATICAL PROBLEMS IN SOCIOLOGICAL LANGUAGE

The problem of vagueness, contradiction, or opacity in grammatical devices per se is not a salient one for sociology. Sociologists are no better and no worse at being grammarians in this sense than any other specialists. However, the failure of grammar to inhibit these general language problems is not so easily pushed aside with respect to sociological language usage.

A highly formalized type of systematization would be necessary to deal with the vagueness, ambiguity, opacity, and contradiction in the core terminology of sociology. Although some steps are being taken in this direction (notably the development of mathematical models and the emphasis on axiomatizing social theories—see Chapter 4), the standard grammatical devices of conventional language are thought to be sufficient for sociological language. As has been demonstrated, these devices are insufficient to compensate for the ambiguity, vagueness, opacity, and contradiction in sociological language.

For other examples, consider these statements: "Landlords owning property near crowded army camps may, for substandard housing, charge the dependents of mobilized soldiers much higher rents than those commonly collected in their region. Are they merely following the accepted business practice, or is their action a deviation from moral norms?" (Inkeles, 1964: 80). The author is asking a rhetorical question to point out the problem of definition of "social deviance." He is implying that whether this case is one of an accepted practice or of a deviant action is a matter of evaluation and context. Now that I have given him his due, let me say that the question is misleading at best. The disjunction "or" implies that the complex object predicates "accepted business practice" and "deviation from moral norms" are or can be considered mutually exclusive attributes of the described activity. When these object predicates are themselves specified by sets of object predicates it would seem most likely that what are instances of one are also instances of the other (the sets intersect). Therefore, the disjunction (grammatical device) "or" malfunctions in this example not only to permit semantic vagueness to occur but also to imply that there is no semantic vagueness occurring: double jeopardy.

Likewise, any time an ambiguous word is used in a sociological statement, and the range of its ambiguity is not delimited by the grammar of that statement, the grammar is functioning deficiently. This should be sufficiently clear. Garfinkel (1967: 57) provides a good contemporary example:

Whatever other determinations an event of everyday life may exhibit. . . . if and only if the event has for the witness the enumerated determinations is it an event in an environment "known in common with others!"

Having read this statement, the reader would anticipate that "the enumerated determinations" would be highly precise because the grammatical equivalence relation "if and only if" suggests such precision. However, this is not the case. On the preceding two pages Garfinkel lists these determinations. They include highly vague and ambiguous terms and statements: e.g., "the determinations are required as matters of 'objective necessity' or 'facts of nature' " vs. "that a relationship of undoubted correspondence is the sanctioned relationship between the-presented-appearance-of-the-object and the-intended-object-that-presents-it-self-in-the-perspective-of-the-particular-appearance" (p. 55). Given the reams of research into the semantics of "necessity" and "fact" and the corresponding delimitation of their multiple meanings, the first statement is ambiguous. On the other hand, it is clear that the meanings of the second statement need to be specified, hence, its vagueness. So in this example, the grammar permits ambiguity and vagueness.

What has been said of grammatical vagueness and ambiguity is equally true of grammatical contradication in sociological language. This analysis is a straightforward extension.

SYSTEMATICALLY MISLEADING EXPRESSIONS IN SOCIOLOGY

Both types of systematically misleading expressions flourish in sociological language. With respect to the first type, consider the following statements: "the doctor's role is . . ."; "the social structure of the group is characterized by . . ."; "a social system is an interdependent set of social units." Statements like these that employ the extralogical terms "role," "social structure," and "social system" as nominals are to be found throughout the sociological literature. Yet these statements (and any similar to them) are systematically misleading expressions of the first type. All three terms are predicative expressions that characterize certain specific examples of human behavior. They do not refer to any unique empirical phenomena. Thus, a doctor exhibits certain characteristic behaviors that may be called his "role," a certain previously specified number of individuals which is called a "group" exhibits certain specified regular and recurrent behaviors which may be called its "social structure," and units A, B, and C (which must be specified) are interconnected in X, Y, and Z ways (which must be specified) and, given these interrelations, can be called a "social system." The basic point is that "role," "social structure," and "social system" are descriptive predicative expressions that must be used as such.

Similarly, such terms as "institutions," "social organization," "status," "cooperation," "equilibrium," "conflict," etc., if they are to form part of the terminology of a scientific language, must never stand in such a nominal position that their inherent predicative function is disguised. In this sense, furthermore, one should not compound the error by qualifying these misplaced or misused nominals as though they were empirical realities. Sociologists speak of "statuses" as positions in "groups" or "the family institution" as being the "core of society," for example. Any sociologist could readily think of dozens of other examples. This mistake is made so often in sociological language usage that it can hardly be overemphasized. Most of the core terms of sociology are actually terms predicated on some form of human behavior and therefore should never be used in a nominal position without, at least, explicit recognition of their actual function. There are no observable empirical events that a hearer or reader could point to when given terms like "status," "role," "institution," etc., unless these terms have previously been predicated on some form of human behavior that is observable. Most sociological statements using such terms as nominals satisfy this minimal condition by the use of examples or illustrations: "The doctor's role consists of such behaviors as wearing a white coat, examining patients, and the like. The doctor's role is instrumental, other-oriented, and affectively neutral." Even when this minimal condition is satisfied, however, one often finds that subsequent statements containing these terms are systematically misleading because the prior specification of the referential meaning of the term has been insufficient and the term is being illegitimately used as a nominal in subsequent contexts.

Similarly, the second form of systematically misleading expression is common in sociological language. The above examples are as much examples of misused "the" phrases as they are of disguised predicative expressions. However, one need not search far for other examples. The title of Durkheim's *The Elementary Forms of the Religious Life* (1965) is an excellent example of misused "the" phrases. There are no such things as "elementary forms of the religious life." This expression must be predicated by extensive reference to observable human behavior, relations, or artifacts before it can be said to refer to empirical events. With a "the" phrase the reader gets the mistaken impression that there must be unique empirical events designated by the phrase when this is not the case. Examples of this type of systematically misleading expression are easily found in sociology.

If the above-declared opacity of some of the most frequently used and well-ensconced terms of sociology violates the reader's intuitive senses, a simple test will assure him of its veracity. When I present a word let the reader think of or imagine an observable occurrence, event, or object that is *the* referent for the particular word. Imagining or thinking of other words is not permissible. Ready? Begin! Status; role; social act; social space; organization; institution; social structure; power; authority; group; social system; norm; social bond; cooperation; bureaucracy. If the reader can immediately bring to mind empirical, observable "things" that can be called the complete referent for these terms, then they can be legitimately used as unqualified nominals in the sociological language system. I assume the reader is incapable of so doing and, hence, that such terms are more precisely used as abstractions or inferences predicated on some form of observable human behavorial event.

Effects of Contextual Meaning

The overall effect of contextual meaning is to produce ambiguity, vagueness, or contradiction. That this is the case should be apparent. It is noteworthy that contextual meaning can function similarly to the above "systematically misleading expressions" in giving opaque words apparent referential meaning. This occurs when an opaque term acquires one or more object predicates through association with a non-opaque term. Consider, for example, the following two statements: "The clug had a vappy. And when a clug has a vappy, that's great." Casting aside any consideration of grammatical meaning, it is clear that the phrase, "that's great," transfers some amount of meaning (albeit un-specified) to the two opaque nonsense syllables "clug" and "vappy."

The high level of vagueness, ambiguity, opacity, and contradiction tolerated in sociological language is compounded by the interacting ef-fects that the transfer of meaning through context has upon these problems. If a significant number of sociology's core extralogical terms are subject to these problems, then the problems must be compounded when such terms are placed in juxtaposition within the context. This point is most in evidence in extended statements that try to clarify an initial sociological term by reference to other sociological terms. "A set of institutions constitutes a 'social system', of which the institutions may be thought of as sub-systems. The term 'social system', like many others in sociology, is used to describe quite different levels of com-plexity" (Inkeles, 1964: 68). The purpose of the above two statements is to effect a transfer of implied object predicates (to exploit contextual meaning, as it were) from all those extralogical terms in the statements that are placed in an identity relation (explicitly or implicitly) with the term "social system." What is actually happening is that opaque and vague terms are used to qualify one another, so that the opacity con-tinues to persist undetected because of a transfer of specifiable predi-cates to the opaque terms. In the phrase, "a set of institutions," the vague term "set," which presumably has acquired specifiable object predicates for the reader because of his familiarity with it, is used to qualify (in this case, to quantify) the opaque term "institution," thereby falsely creating the impression that the latter does have empiri-cally accessible referents. This entire phrase is then placed in an implicit identity relation ("constitutes . . .") with the term "social system" in the obvious hope that the latter will acquire transferred meaning from the former. But the point is that this objective cannot be accomplished by placing "social system" in such a relationship with opaque and vague terms. At best, "social system" acquires a vague meaning; at worst, it acquires opacity of its own. This situation is not rectified by the statements that follow it. Consider the phrase, "of which the insti-tutions may be thought of as sub-systems." The opaque term "institu-tions" is again given implicit quantification by reference to an implied ordering ("sub-") and numeration ("systems"). But these implications are themselves predicated by an opaque term, "system," that *cannot* be justified as having been adequately specified by reference to empirically accessible object predicates. In this important sense, the phrase conveys no new information, for opaque terms ("social system" and "institutions") are qualified by their equivalents ("institutions" and "sub-systems"). The only added feature consists of vague quantifying terms: "set," "sub-," "systems." The second statement does not help to clarify the situation. The phrase, "the term 'social system' " is predicated by "is used to describe quite different levels of complexity." The basic problem with this is that the opaque term, "social system," is given an extremely vague linguistic function ("to describe quite different levels of complexity") which is supposed to help the reader further understand its meaning. However "quite different levels of complexity" is so vague that all that is accomplished is the further legitimation of the usage of an opaque term. Certainly, the term itself has not been more precisely specified.

Scientific vs. Conventional Language Usage. An Elaboration

THE TOLERANCE OF AMBIGUITY, VAGUENESS, OPACITY AND CONTRADICTION

The distinction between conventional and scientific language usage presented in the preceding chapter can now be elaborated. Vagueness, ambiguity, contradiction, and opacity all occur in conventional language. Of the four types of language problems, vagueness is the one most often noted in this respect (see Skinner, 1957; Quine, 1960; Scriven, 1958). In fact, it has been pointed out that vagueness actually serves the valuable linguistic functions of the development of new word forms and the formulation and reformulation of ill-defined concepts (Quine, 1960; Scriven, 1958). A concept may be introduced via a vague term and then gradually developed and made more precise through usage. The point is that vague terms are the only media through which such incomplete concepts may be introduced. Similar types of arguments can be made in favor of the other kinds of linguistic problems.

Moreover, these problems are tolerated in conventional usage because of the large margin of error permissible in the agreements made between users of conventional language. The degree of precision required in conventional language has rather large tolerance limits. Highly connotative words are used freely in conversation. Furthermore, as Chomsky (1965) and Katz (1964a) point out, strict adherence to grammatical rules and forms is more the exception than the rule. Incomplete and ungrammatical utterances are so common in everyday conventional language usage that attempts are now being made to formulate and extend the traditional conceptualization of grammar to explain and describe these phenomena. Thus both semantic and grammatical agreement * seem to be attained less strictly and more easily in conventional than in scientific language usage.

This is not to say, however, that these linguistic problems are allowed free rein in conventional language. Mechanisms exist for their control. The most pervasive such mechanism is linguistic feedback in a psycholinguistic context. Thus, when speaker A uses a vague word and attains a low level of semantic agreement with listener B, listener B will probably ask for a clarification. His medium for so doing can take many forms—questions, declarative sentences, imperatives—but the basic function of such linguistic feedback is to get speaker A to restate and reformulate his initial statement so as to increase the level of semantic agreement attained with listener B. Similar mechanisms exist for the attainment of tolerable levels of grammatical agreement as well. Again, it is noteworthy that definition is a control device that is common in conventional language usage, but that its use is less systematic than in scientific language usage. Also, note that whatever the form of control device used, it operates quite informally in psycholinguistic contexts and not as a component of any highly formalized metalanguage.

Because of the restriction of empirical utility, scientific language usage cannot permit such wide tolerance limits in semantic and grammatical agreement. This does not mean, however, that the above linguistic problems do not occur in scientific language, for elements of

---

* It should be noted that this looser demand for grammatical precision has the reciprocal effect of increasing the probability of occurrence of all the forms of linguistic problems mentioned in the previous section.

vagueness, ambiguity, opacity, and even contradiction cannot be entirely eliminated from any language system. It does mean that the demand for precision is greater, that the level of precision tolerated is higher, and that the requisite control procedures or mechanisms utilized to satisfy both these conditions are more systematically and pervasively used in scientific than conventional language usage.

LEVELS OF PRECISION AND THE OBJECTIVES OF SCIENCE

Scientific language requires greater precision of usage than conventional language because of the different objectives of each. Generally, conventional language requires the understandability of its component terms and statements whereas scientific language requires explanation, prediction, or control of empirical events. Conventional language does not operate under the restriction of empirical utility. Obviously, this is a flexible criterion that can be met within tolerance limits of semantic, grammatical, and contextual agreement, and hence low levels of precision.

It is necessary to distinguish between the more stringent objectives of scientific language use, for each varies in its demands upon language precision. Explanation and prediction can be considered to be synonymous, although this oversimplifies a centuries-old philosophical debate. The prediction of empirical events demands the "confirmability" (after Carnap) of any object designated by any empirically accessible object predicate in a predictive statement. Carnap's definition of "confirmability" is analogous to my previous definition of "agreement." Two (or more) observers must agree with predictable accuracy (which implies predictable margins of error) to the occurrence or nonoccurrence, or the existence or nonexistence, of a designated object, property, or relation at a specified point in time. Confirmability, or agreement, does not impose the restriction of the manipulation of empirical events. Hence, if one's objective is prediction, he need not experimentally control empirical events; all he need do is check his predictions against naturally occurring empirical events through controlled and reliable observation.

The control of empirical events, on the other hand, demands the manipulation of observables, and this in turn requires the "realizability" (Carnap's term: 1953) of any object designated by object predicates in a predictive statement. Carnap defines realizability as the capability of the researcher to produce the object(s) designated in the prediction. If the researcher is so capable, he can proceed to "test" his predictions experimentally, i.e., he can manipulate his independent variables under experimentally controlled conditions.

Philosophers of science disagree as to the necessity for a theory to meet the "control" criterion before it can be rated as a Theory. Astronomy obviously has developed a sophisticated theory without satisfying this criterion. Similarly, evolutionary theory has been of considerable utility without having provided for the direct control of life (although this possibility may soon be realized). Sidestepping this knotty problem, it should be emphasized that explanation or prediction requires less precision of language usage than control, but that both operate under the demands of empirical utility. Moreover, given the criterion of empirical utility, prediction or control as the possible alternative objectives of scientific language use require precision greater than understandability.

SOCIOLOGICAL LANGUAGE AS CONVENTIONAL LANGUAGE

Sociological language more closely approximates conventional than scientific language. The tolerance limits of semantic, grammatical, and contextual ambiguity, vagueness, opacity, and contradiction are simply too lax to permit its designation as a scientific language system. Furthermore, these low levels of precision are permissible and continue because sociologists are generally satisfied with fulfilling the least stringent criterion of understandability. It is only within the last two decades that sociologists have begun to impose predictive form on their statements, and these attempts are faulty in ways that will be examined in Chapter 4.

Emphasis upon this criterion has not only been a sin of omission but also one of commission: there are many sociologists who would maintain that out of either necessity or desirability sociology should be satisfied with understandability as its objective. In certain instances this counterargument is the result of the failure by its proponents to adequately distinguish between understandability and explanation. One can understand the terms and statements of sociological language without direct observation of the empirical events these terms and statements are supposed to designate. Thus, sociologists can agree that the "military-industrial complex" is formed by the interrelationships between certain "institutions and organizations" without ever observing or in any other way directly dealing with the empirics in question. Explanation, on the other hand, requires at some point the observation of the empirical events designated by its component terms and statements. If sociologists speak of "institutions and organizations" in explanations they must at some point refer to the empirics designated by these terms and therefore must have observed or directly dealt with these empirics. Given this distinction, there would probably be few sociologists who would question the necessity of the criterion of explanation or prediction for sociological theory. For those sociologists who would still maintain that sociology should only be concerned with understandability, all that can be said is that they must then be satisfied with the status of a conventional language system for sociological language.

Sociological language is more like a conventional language system also in the efficacy of the language control procedures it employs. It will be remembered that these procedures consist of definition and systematization.

The Efficacy of Language Control Procedures

DEFINITIONAL PROBLEMS: AMBIGUITY, VAGUENESS, CONTRADICTION, OPACITY

Generally, any definition, as the specification of meaning, is subject to vagueness, ambiguity, opacity, and contradiction. A vague definition of an extralogical term is one in which there are multiple specifiable, equiprobable predicates for that term. A vague definition leaves many object predicates unspecified and therefore specifiable. The specification of these object predicates is both necessary and sufficient to attain a tolerably high level of precision in the use of the term. Moreover, with a vague definition no definitional rule has been stated for the ascertainment of permissible specifiable object predicates, and hence there are no definitional criteria for the relative ordering of these specifiable object predicates. An ambiguous definition of an extralogical term is one in which there are multiple, specified, equiprobable object predicates for that term. In any one context in which the term occurs, any of the defining predicates are equally likely to be interpreted as *the* defining predicate for that term. This is to say that the object predicates are specified, but no definitional rule is stated for their relative ordering. A contradictory definition involves the specification of two, equiprobable, logically inconsistent object predicates for an extralogical term. Finally, an opaque definition involves the failure to specify empirical referents for an extralogical term that has been conceptualized as standing in a definable or defined relationship with empirical referents. The definition of the term specifies no object predicates whose validity of application can be ascertained by locating empirical phenomena designated by the object predicates.

Any of these definitional problems can be generated through the use of a definitional rule of exclusion to specify the object predicates forming the referential meaning set of a term: "A is not B, not C, and not D." Hence the traditional injunction against such definitional forms (see Cohen and Nagel, 1934). This can occur when the rule of exclusion is insufficient to specify one predicate or a set of predicates. Thus, ambiguity would arise when all but several specified, equiprobable object predicates are excluded from the definition; vagueness when all but several specifiable, equiprobable predicates are excluded from the definition; contradiction when all but two equiprobable, logically inconsistent object predicates are excluded from the definition; opacity, when all those object predicates that designate empirical phenomena are excluded from the definition and the term is used as if it had object predicates that designated empirical phenomena.

DEFINITIONAL PROBLEMS IN SOCIOLOGY

Blumer (1954) makes the point that explicit definition is sparse in sociological language, and that when definition occurs, it is usually by example. Even when explicit definitions are formulated, they are often vague, ambiguous, contradictory, or opaque in and of themselves. The following example is sufficient to demonstrate this point:

According to Parsons' schema, all social systems must solve four basic problems: (1) adaptation: the accommodation of the system to the reality demands of the environment coupled with the active transformation of the external situation; (2) goal achievement: the defining of objectives and the mobilization of resources to attain them; (3) integration: establishing and organizing a set of relations among the member units of the system that serve to coordinate and unify them into a single entity; and (4) latency: the maintenance over time of the system's motivational and cultural patterns. [Blau and Scott, 1962: p. 38]

Note that the term "social system" as used in this context forms part of a systematically misleading expression: it is opaque in this sense. I point this out for the sake of continuity.

I should like to consider the set of definitions per se. The general point is that these definitions are presented as sufficient in form and content when they are not. They are riddled with opaque, vague and ambiguous defining terms and object predicates. In all four definitions I would classify the following terms and phrases as opaque: "system", "reality demand", "external situation", "mobilization", "units", "serve", "single entity". I would classify the following terms and phrases as vague: "accommodation", "environment", "coupled", "active transformation", "the defining of objectives", "resources", "to attain them", "establishing and organizing", "a set", "among", "member", "to coordinate and unify", "maintenance over time", "motivational and cultural patterns". Insofar as there has been a vast literature on "motivational and cultural patterns" in an attempt to specify their "meanings", these terms are more ambiguous than vague. Finally, definition (3) in its entirety is a disguised version of the "*sui generis* fallacy" and is therefore semantically contradictory. Given the extensive use of these imprecise terms (in every sense of the word), these definitions are extremely imprecise (in every sense of the word). In fact, instead of clarifying the nominals to be defined, these definitions actually compound the problem of their explicit definition by introducing opaque, vague, ambiguous, and contradictory terms into a language system with its fair share of such terms.

The action or relation words in 'the above definitions are an especially interesting case of vagueness (and, possibly, of ambiguity). For example, the terms "accommodation," "coupled," and "maintenance over time" are relational in nature: they refer to processes or events that affect an (assumed to be) empirical entity (or entities). However, their exact components remain specifiable. For the terms to be specified, the object predicates will be conditional and will make reference to spatio-temporal referents as well as to object predicates that are properties of empirical events, and are empirical events. Furthermore, their sufficient specification must make use of multiple conditional and other compound as well as simple object predicates, with this multiplicity being ordered by the general use of disposition predicates specifying relative context. For example, "accomodation" can be specified sufficiently by a definitional chain of the following general form: "If empirical event X_1 occurs at T_1 in space or situation Y_1 and affects empirical event Z_1 in observable ways A_1, B_1 and C_1, and if empirical event X_2 occurs at T_2 in space or situation Y_2 and affects empirical event Z_2 in observable ways A_2, B_2, and C_2, and if empirical event X_3 . . . through a finite and specified series of events [etc.], then 'accommodation' can be said to have taken place." The same is true of the other relational words in the above definition.

Dimensions of Definition: Completeness, Incompleteness, Substitutivity, and Eliminability

Aristotle proposed that all good definitions should be complete. In terms consistent with the prior analysis in this book, all good definitions should exhaustively present the set of object predicates that is a term's referential meaning. If a definition is complete, then the set of object predicates can be freely substituted for the term they define in all contexts in which that term is used. However, contemporary philosophers of science question the possibility of applying these stringent criteria. Kaplan (1946), Scriven (1958), and Northrop (1947), among others, maintain that there is no such thing as a complete definition. Their argument is two-fold. First, since no description of empirical events can be complete, it is impossible that any definition of a term that designates empirical events can be complete. Second, every term serves a linguistic function in a given language system; as the use of that term changes, so must the definition of the term, thereby prohibiting the formation of any one complete definition of the term.

If no definition can be complete, then the free substitution of the defined term by the defining object predicates across contexts is not legitimate. Scriven (1958) offers the less rigid alternative of "eliminability": the defining object predicates must be comprehensible independently of the term they define. This requires the previous existence and linguistic functioning of the predicates so that they have attained at least a minimum level of precision of usage independently of their precision as object predicates in the particular definition.

Sociologists rarely deal with these crucial issues of completeness or incompleteness and substitutivity or eliminability. More often than not, implicitly and through the omission of counterargument they assume their definitions to be complete. This implies that the defined term and its defining predicates can legitimately be substituted for one another. When the object predicates are ambiguous, vague, opaque, or contradictory, they gain entrance into sociological language because they can (presumably) be substituted for the term they define. Again, examples are easily found in sociology. "Emergent properties are essentially relationships between elements in a structure" (Blau, 1964: 3). "Elements in a structure" is a vague phrase that gains access to sociological language through this implicitly complete definition and the principle of substitutivity. Or consider this implicit definition: "The tradition-directed person takes his signals from others, but they come in a cultural monotone; he needs no complex receiving equipment to pick them up" (Riesman, 1961: 25). The use of metaphor for the defining predicates of "tradition-directed person" should be testimony enough to the vagueness and ambiguity of these predicates. Again, the store of vague and ambiguous terms in sociological language is increased through the principle of substitutivity. Instances of this problem are legion in sociology.

Furthermore, even if one accepts the less stringent criterion of eliminability, few sociological definitions could satisfy it because the defining predicates usually are as ambiguous, vague, opaque, and contradictory as the terms they define. Their comprehensibility, apart from the defined term, is therefore open to question. Or more specifically, their independent comprehensibility is dubious when the objectives are explanation or control.

Types of Definitions

THE MISUSE OF NOMINAL DEFINITION IN SOCIOLOGY

Nominal definition is definition by agreement: the users of a term agree that a particular set of predicates are the most appropriate defining predicates of a term. Any discussion of nominal definitions usually compares them with real definitions by way of clarification. Real definition is definition by reference to empirics: the defining predicates of a term are *the* definition of the term because they designate the empirical events that the term is used to designate. There is, then, an arbitrary element in the formation of nominal definitions that is missing with real definitions. The rules of formation are more flexible for nominal definition than for real definition.

However, this distinction has been overemphasized by sociologists (see, Bierstedt, 1959; Zetterberg, 1965). The difference between the two is one of degree rather than kind. There are few purely nominal definitions because there is usually a good reason why language users agree to define a term with a particular set of predicates. This reason usually has something to do with empirical events in one of two ways. First, the defined term usually designates, albeit indirectly, certain empirical events that the defining predicates describe—albeit incompletely and indirectly. Second, the agreement to place certain predicates in a definitional relation with a term is usually contingent upon well-established rules concerning the use of the term. These rules of use form the empirical basis for the particular nominal definition.

One version of sociologists' belief that this distinction is relative can be called the "nominalist fallacy". It has to do with the following argument, advanced by some sociologists. A researcher is definitely under the obligation to define his terms explicitly, but all that is necessary beyond this is that his research remain consistent with the definitions he offers. Otherwise, he may define his terms in the ways he deems most appropriate for these research endeavors. This argument is fallacious because it overlooks the constraints placed upon all definition formation. Any definition is only as good as its empirical utility in a theory language. This utility has two dimensions. First, the defined term must be used to facilitate the formation and derivation of theoretical statements that enhance explanation of the phenomena in question. Second, those terms that are defined must designate or be used to permit the designation of recurrent, stable, and discriminable empirical objects, properties, or relations. This is true in the sense that any theory must be empirically useful: it must predict and explain selected empirical phenomena. These two constraints reduce the degree of freedom in the formation of nominal definition. Against those committed to the "nominalist fallacy" is the fact that there are limits to the arbitrariness of nominal definition formation.

This confusion among sociologists about nominal vs. real definitions has had two negative effects. First, the extreme arbitrariness in definition formation, coupled with the assumed completeness of these definitions and the principle of substitutivity, has led to the introduction and use of ambiguous, vague, opaque, and contradictory terms in sociological language. Second, many sociological terms whose lack of precision should have been cause enough for their deletion have survived because they were given nominal definitions. Excessively vague, ambiguous, opaque, and contradictory terms have found their way into honored positions in the core terminology of sociology because their nominal definitions conferred legitimacy upon them. In my opinion, an excellent example is "social structure." Usually defined as "the patterned relations between men," it is a favorite sociological term. I have two objections to its use. First, it conveys the impression that sociologists are dealing with phenomena that have the stability of the phenomena of the physical sciences. The word "structure" implies the existence of perceptual wholes like buildings or cars or chairs when in actuality the parameters of social phenomena are not as easily extrapolated from the empirics of human behavior. Secondly, the compound predicate "the patterned relations between men" is freely substitutable for "social structure." The predicate, although in need of extensive definition, directs one's attention to the phenonema one is to study while suggesting the complexity of these phenomena. This compound predicate should replace the term rather than being used as a nominal definition to maintain the misleading term in sociological language.

THE MISUSE OF OSTENSIVE DEFINITION BY SOCIOLOGISTS

Ostensive definition has traditionally been considered to include definition by pointing or other types of indication as well as definition by example. I shall consider definition by example only.

Sociologists often rely on definition-by-example as a technique for introducing new terms into their language system. "A status is a position in a social group or grouping, in relation to other positions held by other individuals in the same group or grouping. Some polar sta-

tuses are father-child, employer-employee, priest-parishioner, govern-
ment official-citizen, and gang leader-gang member" (Green, 1960: 45);
or "conflict is the deliberate attempt to oppose, resist, or coerce the
will of another or others . . . a conscientious objector who refuses to
fight is involved in conflict as surely as the bayonet-wielding infantry-
man" (Green, 1960: 60). Such ostensive definition is insufficient. It is of
utility in introducing these terms into sociological language but at a
level of precision that is equivalent to conventional rather than scientific language usage. Its overall effect in the above two examples is to
legitimate the initial nominal definitions that are riddled with ambiguity, vagueness, contradiction and opacity. Are social groups equivalent
to geographical areas and statuses in them equivalent to relative positions in these areas? Why did the theorist deem it necessary to say
"group or grouping"; what is the difference between the two? Does
the specification of status as "a position in relation to other positions"
in a group convey sufficient information so that the referent of "status"
is easily discriminable and observable? Is not this specification equivalent to saying a "status is something that stands in relation to other statuses" with the criterial attributes and relations involved never actually
being specified? Likewise, what is a "deliberate attempt"? What does,
"to oppose, resist, or coerce the will of another or others" actually
mean? How does one observe "wills" when philosophers and theolo-
gians have argued about their existence for centuries? Can "conflict"
be defined as a process apart from some specification of those engaging
in it? Is "conflict" an observable thing or a series of observable events
occurring over time? If I wanted to deliberately "attempt to oppose,
resist, or coerce the will of another or others," just what would I do?
Questions such as these (and there are many more that could be posed)
should demonstrate the inadequacy of the above definitions in terms of
precision. Yet, these two definitions are buttressed by examples that
follow them and hence given sufficient credibility and precision to
make them understandable. Their ostensive counterparts give the
reader just enough information so that he can say to himself, "Well,
the definition leaves me a little uneasy, but these examples help clarify
things a bit." The examples put him enough at ease so that he can use
the terms "conflict" and "status" in statements understandable to others, or at least he is himself capable of understanding statements con-

taining such terms. Hence, the level of precision at which these terms are introduced into the sociological language system is equivalent to the level of precision of a conventional language system. Therefore, such ostensive definition, in effect, legitimates the introduction and use of low-precision terms in the sociological language system.

Systematization: General Problems in Sociology

As I have previously mentioned, systematization is similar to grammar in its functioning. I have meant to use it as a broader concept than grammar so that it includes not only standard grammatical devices, but also the formalization of extended theoretical statements by use of such devices as axiomatization and mathematical model building. There are two general points I wish to make about the use of systematization as an error control device in sociological language.

First, the attempts at theory formalization in sociology that have recently come to the fore (i.e., axiomatization and model building) almost always overlook the problems of sociological language per se and proceed to specify the relations and forms of relations between core and peripheral sociological terms, taking these terms as given. It is true that systematization has only a tangential and indirect bearing on the precision of semantic usage. It is basically concerned with the precision of syntactic or grammatical usage. Therefore, the systematization in sociological language that is gaining momentum (for example, see Zetterberg, 1956; Gross, 1959; Homans, 1964; Blalock, 1964; and Simon, 1957) is only a partial answer to the problems of this language system. Moreover, it can have the disastrous effect of misdirecting attention away from the crucial problems, and focusing it upon problems that can be answered at some later time after these crucial problems have been answered. This is to say that such endeavors may in actuality be putting the cart before the horse. I shall elaborate this point in Chapter 4 when considering the general efficacy of systematization as one possible solution to the problems in sociological language.

Second, much of sociological language at present makes use of conventional grammar as a systematizing control device. This standard device is clearly insufficient and inefficient. As mentioned above, the restrictions placed on sociological terminology by conventional grammar are clearly insufficient to handle the language problems of sociology, and they may and often do compound these problems.

Summary

Sociological language, then, is a conventional language system. It has component terms that are excessively vague, ambiguous, opaque, and contradictory. It does not have adequate control devices to cope with these general language problems.

There are four general language problems. Vagueness exists when a term or expression has multiple, equiprobable, *specifiable* referential meanings. Ambiguity exists when a term or expression has multiple, equiprobable, *specified* referential meanings. Opacity exists when a term or expression has no referential meaning. Contradiction exists when a term or expression has logically inconsistent referential meanings.

Sociology is peculiarly subject to these problems. Grammar sometimes functions so as to be subject to these problems or to permit them in the terms or expressions of statements. The latter difficulty is relevant for sociology both in terms of the "bad" use of grammar, the ingrained "*sui generis* fallacy," and the extensive use of "systematically misleading expressions." Contextual meaning usually contributes to these general language problems. This is quite true in sociology. Scientific language tolerates less of these problems than conventional language. In this sense, sociology is more like a conventional than scientific language system.

A scientific language system also makes rigorous use of two language control procedures: definition and systematization. This is not true of a conventional language system. Sociologists use vague, ambiguous, opaque, and contradictory definitions. Furthermore, they misuse the completeness-substitutivity assumption so as to introduce problematic terms into their language system. They also misuse nominal and ostensive definition so as to introduce problematic terms into their language and to legitimate problematic (defined) terms. Finally, sociologists use

Ideally, a theorist should specify the epistemic correlations linking particular operations with some of his theoretical concepts. . . . but this is obviously expecting too much, given the present status of most social sciences. Since there is a wide variety of possible research designs, measurement instruments, and compounding factors, it is much more reasonable to work out a division of labor in the process of theory construction. . . . [He then goes on to elaborate on the form of the "general theory"] In the process of *constructing* such a theory, the social scientist need not be concerned with the method of testing his propositions or even with specifying populations for which the theory should apply. This is not to say, however, that the theory may not have been *suggested* by empirical data appropriate to particular populations. [1968: 24–25]

Thus, what is at best a heuristic distinction between a theory language and an object language becomes a program for conducting social scientific research. Its adoption as a fundamental truth has the empirical consequences of dualizing the sociologist's (or social scientist's) research endeavors.

Despite the apparent contemporary emphasis upon "proposition formation and hypotheses testing" the old conflict between theory building and empiricism continues in the modern guise of an assumed gap between two aspects of any theoretical system. This is not to say that all sociologists are guilty of this, only that it has become a pervasive enough trend in sociology to deserve consideration. For a contemporary example see Willer and Webster, 1970.

The history of natural science has demonstrated over and over again that the most productive theories have been developed by researchers who were concerned with a finite set of problems in one area of endeavor, who were dually engaged in the process of inductively building theories and deductively-inductively testing them, and who repeatedly and continuously engaged in the inductive and deductive processes of theorizing and research (see Kemeny, 1959). It is strange that a discipline which draws numerous analogies and comparisons to the natural and physical sciences has not learned this lesson.

Inasmuch as the heuristic concept of the dual nature of a theory becomes a research program for sociologists, thereby dividing their endeavors, this most fruitful program for research and theory building will not be used. That this is the case is well known by those conversant with the field: there are theory builders and technicians, specialists in theory and specialists in methodology, macro-level research and micro-level research (although this distinction only partially reflects the distinction between a theory language and an object language), social organization experts and researchers and small group experts and researchers (again only a partial reflection of the above), and "think pieces" vs. "research pieces" in terms of published material. In my opinion, it is this schism and the failure to make use of the tried and true theory-building strategy of the other sciences that has had the greatest determining effect in retarding sociology's development as a science.

The Faulty Use of Primitive Terms in Sociology

To reiterate, two kinds of primitive or undefined extralogical terms are permissible in any theory. The first type consists of those terms that occur at the upper levels of generality in a theory. These terms are not explicitly defined but are implicitly defined by their functional importance in the theory. They can be defined by using some form of conditional object predicates that specify their use in the component theoretical statements of the theory. I shall call these "abstract primitives." The second type consists of those object predicates and terms that purportedly stand in a one-to-one correspondence with observable objects, properties, or relations. These need not be defined because they, in effect, are the symbolic representatives of certain perceptual realities. I shall call these terms "simple primitives." This dichotomy parallels the theory language and object language distinction. That is, the theory language has always been believed to be composed of abstract primitives and the object language of simple primitives. However, the dichotomy is not analogous to this distinction because it refers to types of isolated terms and not to types of language systems. Moreover, it makes no assertions about a necessary definitional relation between the two; the point is that abstract primitives do not need definition.

Sociologists misuse both types of primitives. They use terms as abstract primitives when there are no sophisticated bodies of theoretical statements in sociology to legitimate these terms. For example, La Piere (1965) develops a "theory" of "social change" without explicitly defining "social change." Yet, his theory is not a theory in the sense of a formalized body of verifiable theoretical statements. It is rather a narrative, polemical account of certain loosely described phenomena. He is completely unjustified, then, in using "social change" as an abstract primitive. By way of contrast, Sidman (1960), talking about the simpler phenomenon of the change of behavior of organisms, gives an excellent discussion of the actual complexities involved in defining "change": e.g., where are the exact transition points, by what criteria are these selected, etc.?

Similarly, sociologists illegitimately use certain terms as simple primitives. In fact, I know of no sociological term that can qualify as a simple primitive. This is true because all sociological terms must be defined with terminal reference to observable aspects of human behavior. Human behavior is the stuff of every social science: the limited empirical domain that defines the ultimate empirical utility of every theoretical statement in social sciences. There are few sociological terms used as simple primitives that designate directly observable aspects of human behavior. Illustrations of this fact were presented in the last chapter with respect to such terms as "status," "role," "group," etc. Further examples will be presented in the next chapter when Zetterberg's (1963) sets of simple primitive terms are considered. The point is that few sociological terms that are used as simple primitives satisfy the criteria for classification as simple primitives.

The Requisite Designation of Observables

REPORTS VS. BEHAVIOR

Basically, two types of data are examined by sociologists. The first consists of observable aspects of human behavior: those aspects of human behavior that can be perceived directly because they have what sociologists deem to be sufficient spatial and temporal referents. The second consists of reports about observable aspects of human behavior: the spatial and temporal referents of the aspects of human behavior are transmitted via language. Every time a researcher relies on participant or nonparticipant observation, on physiological measuring devices, or on the recording of behavior frequencies or durations, he is dealing with type 1. Every time a researcher takes a survey, uses a questionnaire, gives an interview, or asks a subject about aspects of his behavior, he is dealing with type 2. Language can be treated as type 1, in which case it is called "verbal behavior." Language is also the medium of type 2 and as such is called "reports."

It is sufficient to specify the spatial and temporal referents of the observations in order to record type 1. However, two sets of specifications are necessary for sufficiently recording type 2: specification of the reports and specification of the truth value of the reports. The first is accomplished by coding the questionnaire or interview. The second requires not only truth scales in the questionnaires and interviews but also extensive empirical research into how people use terms to describe their behavior. That is, research is necessary into the use of language by people. Such research would have to answer questions like the following: under what conditions do people lie, exaggerate, supply unnecessary information, falsify, or in any other way distort their reports about their behavior or the behavior of others; what types of questions best tap subjective experiences like emotions, beliefs, and opinions, or, in other words, what terms and statements do people map onto these events; what terms or statements express what degrees of intensity of particular subjective experiences; what is an adequate description of a given event, adequate in the sense that it conveys all the necessary information; what is an adequate explanation of a given event? Without such research, the best instrument used to record reports about human behavior must assume adequate answers to these questions. This obviously poses severe reliability and validity problems. Such is the state of sociological survey research, for these questions have been given no satisfactory empirical answers.

GROUP TERMINOLOGY

"Group terminology," "collective terms," or "institutional concepts" are terms commonly used to refer to those expressions that purportedly designate attributes or relations of collective entities. They are extensively used in sociology. Actually, there are three subtypes of group terms.

The first type may be called "summarizers." These include all those terms that refer to similar properties, behaviors, or relations of individuals. That is, they are defined by sets of object predicates which specify similar properties, behaviors, or relations of individuals. They can refer to the distribution of these similar events across individuals at one point in time or across a limited number of individuals through a period of time. Examples of the first would be statistical indices like "age," "sex," "I. Q.," "occupation," etc. Examples of the second would be terms like "anxiety," "guilt," "fear," etc. Both of these kinds of summarizers are legitimate abstractions in the sense that their referential meanings stay constant within certain tolerable limits. Moreover, they can be precisely defined. All that need be done is the specification of the rule of inclusion governing the object predicates in the referential set.

"Summators" are the second type of group term. They refer to disparate attributes, behaviors, or relations of individuals. They are defined by sets of dissimilar object predicates. Like summarizers, summators can refer to the distribution of these dissimilar observables either across individuals at one time or across a limited number of individuals through time. Examples of the first are terms like "group," "bureaucracy," "society," "institution," "class." Examples of the second are terms like "status," "role," "conflict," "cooperation," "power." These terms require extensive explication and definition before their referential meanings will stay constant. They require extensive definitional chains in order to specify the dissimilar object predicates. Moreover, they are subject to extensive vagueness and ambiguity. Vagueness arises because the use of a definitional rule of inclusion is impossible given the dissimilarity of the object predicates. This means that any definition of these terms must proceed by listing all the relevant object predicates. This task is almost always impossible to accomplish; hence these definitions remain open-ended, and the use of the term necessarily will be vague. These terms are subject to ambiguity because rarely are the dissimilar object predicates ordered.

The third class of group terms can be called "*sui generis* terms." These terms are supposed to refer to collective entities that can be defined without necessary reference to attributes, behaviors, or relations of individuals. There has been extensive sociological and philosophical debate over the legitimacy of these terms (see Blau, 1964; Brodbeck, 1958). If one accepts the tenet that the stuff of sociology is human behavior, and that the empirical utility of any sociological theory will therefore be contingent on the adequate prediction of selected aspects of human behavior, then every term must be directly definable by reference to attributes, behaviors, or relations of human beings. Therefore, *sui generis* terms will have limited utility in any future sociological theory that approximates a scientific language system.

A more stringent argument against these terms is possible. If all group terms must have terminal reference to attributes, behaviors, or relations of individuals, then *sui generis* terms are opaque by definition. The only observables of social life are attributes, behaviors, and relations of individuals. As the only observables, they must be the basic data of any theory purporting to explain social life. For example, any theory of "group behavior" must deal with the attributes, behaviors, and relations of people who make up groups because these are the only perceptual events the theoretician has to deal with. If these are *the* basic data of any possible sociological theory, then any such theory is restricted to using the group terms that refer to these aspects of individuals: i.e., summators and summarizers. Moreover, even those group terms that may legitimately be employed as abstract primitives (and therefore that need not be defined) must function via the restriction of empirical utility to permit the observation and prediction of these aspects of individual human beings. All *sui generis* terms, then, are opaque. One need not accept this more stringent argument against the legitimacy of *sui generis* group terms. The first is sufficient to restrict their use in any sociological theory, and hence to minimize their problematic effects.

Group terminology is the medium of expression for reports about human behavior. This is true in two senses. First, survey researchers employ it as their theory language to describe and explain aspects of type 2 phenomena. Secondly, the reports about human behavior that is composed of type 2 phenomena are usually expressed in group terminology. People usually use this terminology in day-to-day discourse to describe aspects of their lives. Their reports about their behavior naturally tend to be expressed in group terminology. Yet, the use of summators and *sui generis* terms is quite problematic. Insofar as these terms are a reflection of type 2 phenomena, and insofar as survey research deals exclusively with these phenomena, survey research has inherent in it all the problems of group terminology.

THE OMISSION OF CRUCIAL OBJECT PREDICATES

Whether the sociological researcher is dealing with reports about human behavior or with direct observations of human behavior, there is one basic criterion of theoretical adequacy. The particular theory language must exhaustively deal with the phenomena that are the subject matter of the theory. This means that the sets of object predicates must exhaustively cover the domain. Sociological theory is deficient not only in failing to provide an adequate set of object predicates for any of its core terms, but also in omitting certain important object predicates from its theory language.

Sociology avoids the consideration of verbal behavior as a social reality.* Yet, verbal behavior is *the* social reality. Without communication there would be no social life; verbal behavior, therefore, becomes critical in any theory about social behavior. Also of special interest in this respect is the frequent failure of sociologists to take into account the cumulative nature of behavior that is due to memory and other symbolic storing mechanisms like the written word. Without such storing mechanisms and without the verbal and other symbolic media cumulative learning could not occur. Moreover, without these, what are designated "social organizations," "social institutions," and "social structures" would not develop, function, or persist. Therefore, the study of verbal behavior is crucial for sociology, but no systematic, observation-based terminology has been developed in the area.

The same is true of the study of "social change." As this term is presently used it is opaque, vague, or ambiguous depending on the particular sociological theorist using it. A minimal prerequisite for the study of social change is the specification of observable units of analysis and the relevant boundaries of change and nonchange states. It is noteworthy that there are no empirically accessible object predicates in

---

* Some of the work of the "ethnomethodologists" and "exchange theorists" is an exception to this generalization, although this work is frought with the same linguistic and theoretical problems as all sociology. See Chapter 5.

sociological terminology that accomplish this. In fact, there is considerable difficulty in identifying exactly what are the relevant boundaries
of the phenomena, as well as what are the phenomena to be studied.
Which is to say, there is considerable difficulty in defining exactly
what "social change" is (as with La Piere, 1965).

The same is true of sociologists' considerations of physiological variables. Sociologists usually staunchly defend their failure to consider
physiological variables on two grounds. First, there are phenomena
that are peculiarly social to which physiological variables are irrelevant. Second, to consider physiological variables is to deny the existence of social realities; or, to put it differently, such a consideration
overlooks the existence of complex social phenomena that can at best
be only minimally explained by reference to physiological factors.
However, I believe that physiological variables, in addition to being
possible control variables, act as a relative contributor to error in one's
predictions; and that a sociological theoretical language system should
reflect these functions. Therefore, I would question the validity of the
first defense against the use of such terms in sociology as well as the assumption of the second defense that they can only minimally explain
complex social phenomena. This is not to deny the legitimate existence
of complex social phenomena and a theory language relevant to them,
nor, conversely, is it to claim that all sociological variables, terms, and
predictions are ultimately reducible to physiological variables, terms,
and predictions. It does say that physiological variables are legitimate
as a probable source of error and as theoretically fertile and empirically
useful control variables in any and all sociological predictions. (Actually, this approach is more conservative than the traditional sociological approach that stresses the use of such physiological variables as sex
and age as *independent* and *dependent* variables in one's research.)

The following example should clarify this argument. Much work has
been done by sociologists on the social organization of mental hospital
wards. (See Argyris, 1956; Bateman and Dunham, 1948; Brannon, 1947;
Caudill, 1958; Devereaux, 1944 and 1949; Dunham and Weinberg,
1960; Fonseca, 1956; etc.) The drugs given mental patients have crucial
physiological effects on them which are phenotypically manifested in
their overt behavior. It has been my experience that any "old-time" at-
tendant who has worked in mental hospitals both before and after the

introduction of drugs can supply a host of information about the changes that drugs have produced in patient behavior (notably, to make the patient less agitated, extreme, and violent). Insofar as social organization deals with human behavior, these effects on patient behavior must of necessity have relevance for the study of the "social organization" of patient behavior on any mental hospital ward. Yet, none of the sociological studies in this area attempt to specify these relative effects. Drugs and their physiological-behavioral effects are taken as a constant in these studies: they are the base line of observations about social organization among mental patients. This is not legitimate because the physiological effects of the drugs are never constant: they vary with dosage, time elapsed between administrations of dosage, the weight of the patient, the health of the patient, the time of day, and so on. Since these effects are never constant, there can be no constant base line of observation of patient behavior unless these effects are taken into account as probable sources of error and as control variables. This, in turn, necessitates the introduction into the relevant language system of empirically accessible object predicates that designate physiological objects, properties, or relations with respect to patient behavior.

The Necessary Designation of Action Referents

One can make a distinction between the type of concept and corresponding definition needed to designate action referents (type 1 phenomena) and those that are needed to designate other types of referents. Generally, action referents must be designated by some form of "disposition concept," as first defined by Carnap (1956: 63): "Suppose that there is a general regularity in the behavior of a given thing of such a kind that, whenever the condition S holds for the thing or its environment, the event R occurs at the thing . . . we shall say that the thing has the disposition to react to S by R, or for short, that it has the property D_{sr}." Since all forms of human behavior are subsets of action referents, any given instance of behavior would need to be designated by a disposition concept (or in this case, disposition predicate).

This implies several things, given the properties of disposition con-

cepts. First, any extralogical term referring to human behavior should
be specified by a disposition concept containing spatio-temporal referents. For example, one possible way of specifying "Jim fought with
Bill" would be the following: "Jim raised his arm at T_1, lowered it at
T_2 and contacted Bill's face at T_3; Jim was three feet from
Bill at the time; it was inferred that Jim did so out of anger, because
his face was flushed; at T_4 Bill had called Jim a 'son of a bitch.' " Second, a disposition concept can be completely defined by the specification of S and R, which implies the specification of spatio-temporal referents as well. So in the above example, "Jim fought with Bill" has
been completely defined by the specification of Jim's behavior in reaction to Bill's behavior, with all necessary (and assumed sufficient) spatio-temporal referents delineated as well. This type of specification is
therefore necessary and sufficient for the complete definition of any extralogical term referring to human behavior (e.g., "fought," "argued,"
"loved"). Third, multiple disposition concepts can be used to specify
extralogical terms that designate multiple instances of human behavior.
"The multiple disposition concept $D_{s1r1}, D_{s2r2} \ldots, D_{snr_n},$ is the disposition to react to S_1 by R_1, to S_2 by R_2, and finally to S_n, by R_n"
(Carnap, 1956: 64). Since most extralogical terms that refer to human
behavior are general, most of these terms can be defined only through
the use of multiple disposition concepts. This means that the set of defining predicates of such terms will consist of conditional object predicates of disposition form, i.e., they will specify S and R through the
use of spatio-temporal referents. Finally, operational definitions are
used to define disposition concepts when the researcher's theoretical
objectives are observability and testability. Operational definitions are
dispostion concepts in which the researcher or observer produces condition S at will. Furthermore, multiple operational definitions can be
used to define multiple disposition concepts. Since, as I have indicated,
most general extralogical terms with human action referents can be
(and should be) defined by sets of conditional object predicates of disposition form (with all that this implies), it follows that if a researcher's
objectives include the testing of predictions about human behavior
(which implies the control of human behavior), the use of multiple operational definitions would be appropriate. If, on the other hand, a researcher's objectives involve only the formulation of confirmable gen-

eralizations about human behavior, then operational definition can be dispensed with. This is not to say, however, that multiple disposition predicates can be excluded from definitions conforming to such loose standards of theorizing. *Multiple disposition predicates must always be included at some stage of definition formation in theoretical systems that employ general extralogical terms having human action (or behavior) referents.* This is true, despite the relative strictness of the theoretical objectives of the theoretical system involved. The only thing that can be justifiably dispensed with in such systems is operational definition as one possible definitional technique for specifying the disposition predicates. The disposition predicates must always be introduced at some point into the theoretical language involved.

SOCIOLOGY'S FAILURE TO USE DISPOSITION CONCEPTS

Weber (1962a) first noted that the proper subject matter of sociology was human action. As has been mentioned, in the sense that human action and its effects are the only perceptual realities or observables of social life, this argument can be strengthened to read: reports and observations of aspects of human action are the only possible subject matter of sociology. Given what has just been said, this implies the extensive use of disposition concepts by sociologists. Yet, rarely are these employed by sociologists (see Kadushin, 1968, for a noteworthy exception with respect to such a definition of "power"). This serious deficiency is the result of sociologists' failure to deal with an isolated empirical domain.

Types of Predictions

This section will not attempt to exhaust the sundry types of predictions available. It will present a commonly recognized distinction (see Hempel, 1958). Predictions can be divided into two general types on the basis of how strictly they apply to their empirical referents. Universalistic predictions take the form: "All A's are B's" or "all cases of A are cases of B" or "$A_1, A_2, A_3 \ldots A_n$ [including all possible members of finite set A_i] if and only if $B_1, B_2, B_3 \ldots B_n$ [including all possible members of finite set B_i]." Universalistic predictions, then, refer to all the empirical events within their predictive domains. Statistical predications, on the other hand, take the general form: "the probability of an A being a B is 0.50" or "the probability of a case of A being a case of B is 0.99" or any equivalent statement. They do not apply to every empirical event in their predictive domain. To do so the stated probability level would have to be 1.0.

The strength of universalistic predictions is their capacity to generate deductively predictions about individual events. That is, to permit the deduction of predictions that can be unequivocally applied to singular events. Given that "all A's are B's" and that "this is an A", one can deduce that "this is a B." Statistical predictions cannot of themselves be used to generate deductively predictions that can be applied unequivocally to singular events. Given that "the probability of an A being a B is 0.99" (to take the extreme case) and that "this is an A," one cannot deduce that "this is a B," for this instance may be the one time in a hundred that the prediction is inapplicable. In order to deduce the final statement one must supply the buttressing assumption that in this one instance the statistical prediction will apply.

Statistical predictions, then, are phrased so that, of necessity, they will be inapplicable within their domain a certain percentage of the time. This amount of error can be expressed as a proportion, the number of times the prediction is inapplicable within its domain / the total number of applications of the prediction in this domain, or as a ratio, the number of times the prediction does not apply within its domain/the number of times the prediction applies in this domain. Given their phrasing, statistical predictions necessarily will not apply a certain number of times within their domain, and hence they have a certain amount of a priori error built into them.

DO UNIVERSALISTIC PREDICTIONS EXIST?

This question is tantamount to asking, "Are there such things as errorless predictions?" The answer is *no* for several reasons (see Kaplan, 1964 and Kemeny, 1959 on "determinacy" for a more inclusive discussion of this topic).

First of all, no description or definition can be complete. Insofar as this applies to the component extralogical terms embedded in universalistic predictions, it precludes the possibility of forming such statements. One cannot state that "all A's are B's" if not every A and B can be known and designated.

Similarly, every prediction must have error built into it because of the nature of the theory construction process. The core of this process involves the mapping of linguistic and mathematical symbols on to physical events with the subsequent manipulation of the resulting correspondences to predict these physical events. The theoretician knows of these physical events second-hand through his symbols. Such mediated knowledge must be faulty, just as photographs can only be approximate representations of their subject matter.

The famous Heisenberg Principle in nuclear physics demonstrates the veracity of the above statement. This principle states that the position and the velocity of an electron cannot be measured at the same time. If the position is measured the velocity must be distorted, and if the velocity is measured the position must be distorted. This truth has demonstrated the indeterminacy and error that is inherent in all measurement. Measurement is the theoretician's bridge to the physical world. It enters the theory construction process at both its initial phase of the inductive formation of theoretical statements and its terminal phase of the verification of hypotheses deduced from these statements. The theoretical statements, then, cannot be truly universalistic because they must have error built into them with their inductive formation, and they can never be proven universalistic because of verificational error.

Finally, purely universalistic predictions cannot be formulated because of the indeterminacy of inductive logic. Hume (1946) demonstrated the uncertainty and incompleteness of induction. One can observe that "all past and present A's are B's," but one can never know for certain that "all future A's will be B's." One of his examples is more graphic: There is no errorless reason why the sun will rise tomorrow. To say that it must be so because the sun rose yesterday, and the day before, and so on, is insufficient because there are infinite reasons why it may not: e.g., the earth may blow up, the sun may blow up, God may abolish the universe, etc., etc. The crux of the issue is that man can never have complete knowledge because he cannot have complete experience.

However, to say that truly universalistic predictions are impossible is not to deny their utility. In short, they can function as models of optimal prediction for the theoretician. As such, they are the heart of a tried and true research strategy in all the sciences: to posit one's theoretical statements in universalistic form and then to search out the exceptions, subsequently formulating conditional theoretical statements to explain these exceptions. This is the growth mechanism of theories; hence, the functional importance of universalistic predictions.

THE MOST APPROPRIATE PREDICTIVE FORM

Since errorless predictions can be legitimately formulated only as a research and theory-building strategy, the most appropriate predictive form is one that will permit a statement of error. One way of doing this is by the use of the *ceteris paribus* clause. Ploch (1970), for example, suggests that the appropriate predictive form is "*A* if and only if *B*" qualified by the *ceteris paribus* clause, "all other things being equal." This can be questioned on two grounds. First, the biconditional "if and only if" is a form of universalistic prediction and is therefore too stringent to be empirically approximated. Second, the *ceteris paribus* clause is too vague. It does not encourage inquiry into those factors that may cause error in a given prediction. Neither does it supply the appropriate symbolic format for the codification of these possible error-producing factors. Given the low level of precision in sociological theory, both these factors would seem to have negative effects.

A better alternative is the following predictive form:

"If *A* then *B*
Given conditions: 1
                          2
                          .
                          .
                          .
                          n

And possible error, *e*"

The conditional "if . . . then" is not too stringent to be approximated, and the sources of error can be specified by expanding the number of conditions under which the prediction is applicable within its domain. That is, if the prediction is found to be inapplicable within its domain under certain conditions, all that need be done to increase its range of applicability is to specify these conditions. This predictive format would seem to be flexible yet formalized enough to match the elusiveness, lability, and complexity of sociological empirics.

MARGINS OF ERROR

By permitting the exact specification of predictive error this form of prediction can approximate the most precise types of scientific prediction. Since all predictions of necessity must be statistical, their relative precision can be evaluated by how they provide for error. The most precise will specify limits to the error that can be expected: it will attach numerical confidence limits to the number of times it can be expected to be inapplicable. This is the form that the most sophisticated predictions in physics take. The next most precise will provide an open-ended error estimate: it will specify that the prediction will probably be inapplicable within its domain no fewer than N times. The next most precise will provide an error estimate that is not specific: it will assert that the prediction can be expected not to apply in certain instances, and will list several of these instances, but will not specify the expected range. Finally, the least precise will be statistical but will make no provision for error: it will have no error term.

On Sociological Predictions

Sociologists have just begun to codify their theoretical statements in predictive form. Those predictions that do exist are of the lowest level of precision. They either do not specify an error term or they simply tack on an "e" to the statement. Moreover, rarely are these predictions expressed by use of the conditional, in the appropriate way mentioned above. Their usual form is "the greater (less of) X, the greater (less of) Y," or "the more of (less of) X, the more of (less of) Y," or "X varies directly (inversely) with Y." (For example, see Blalock, 1964). Interestingly enough, it is only when they speak abstractly about predictions as mathematical models that sociologists deem it necessary to supply an unspecified error term.

Why this low level of precision in their predictions? Different answers have been offered: the early stage of development of the discipline; the heavy philosophical residue remaining from sociology's historical antecedents; the complexity and lability of sociology's subject matter; an unsophisticated and underdeveloped methodology. All these, of course, are true to varying degrees. Another reason not so commonly mentioned has to do with sociology's problem-ridden language system.

SOCIOLOGICAL PREDICTIONS AND SOCIOLOGICAL LANGUAGE

What happens when vague, ambiguous, contradictory, and opaque terms are placed in predictions? In the answer to this question is one of the major causes of sociology's lack of predictive rigor.

A vague term has multiple specifiable object predicates as its referential meaning. It follows that any statement containing a vague term will have multiple specifiable interpretations; or, in other words, any statement containing a vague term can be translated into multiple, specifiable, alternative statements. Each of these statements will contain one or more of the specifiable object predicates. Of course, before this can be done the particular object predicate(s) must first be specified. However, the range of possible translations will not be known because the component object predicates have not been previously specified. This means that when the statement in which a vague term is embedded is a prediction, the error in that prediction cannot be estimated. If such a prediction has multiple, alternative translations whose range is not known, then the range of application of these derived predictions cannot be known, hence neither can their range of error.

An ambiguous term has multiple specified object predicates as its referential meaning. Therefore, any statement containing an ambiguous term will have multiple, specified interpretations or alternative statements into which it can be translated. The range of possible statements that are derived via translation will be known because the object predicates of the initial term have been specified, and they are the core components of the derived statements. When the initial statement is a prediction, its range of application will be known and its margin of error will be estimable.

The case with opaque and contradictory terms is not as complicated. Since opaque terms do not have any object predicates, they have no connection with empirical events. Therefore, any predictions of which they are components cannot be applied to empirical events and have no truth value, and so the question of error is an academic one. Contradictory terms embedded in predictions generate logical inconsistencies.

Insofar as sociological terms are vague, sociological predictions will have inestimable amounts of error. Insofar as sociological terms are ambiguous, sociological predictions will have estimable amounts of error. Insofar as sociological terms are opaque, sociological predictions will have no truth value. Insofar as sociological terms are contradictory, sociological predictions will be logically inconsistent.

Class 2 Phenomena and Predictive Error

As has been mentioned above, reports about human behavior tend to be expressed in group terminology. Moreover, group terminology tends to be subject to ambiguity, vagueness, opacity, and contradiction. These problems lead to inherent predictive difficulty: estimable error, inestimable error, lack of truth value, and logical inconsistency; hence, the low level of predictive precision in sociology.

STATISTICS AND LACK OF PREDICTIVE RIGOR

A necessary (but not sufficient) way of solving these language problems is through repeated use of the particular terms in question: specifically, through their repeated application to their empirical referents in order to increase agreement as to their usage and hence their level of precision. Analogously, a necessary (but not sufficient) way of decreasing predictive error is through repeated application of particular predictions to the events in their domain. This will permit the assessment of their range of inapplicability and therefore the estimation of the magnitude of their error. In addition, it will permit specification of the conditions that govern their applicability and therefore of the information needed to decrease that range of error. Without this repeated application the predictive error in a theory will remain constant.

The use of inductive statistics has become widespread in sociology. It has two purposes. First, through the medium of probability theory, it provides some model of expected outcomes against which predicted and actual outcomes can be compared. Second, it provides the mathematical techniques needed to make this comparison. The first function is of primary importance here. All predictions will be applicable to the events in their domain only a certain percentage of the time. If a prediction is applied to the events in its domain a finite but large number of times, a distribution of the range of applicability will be obtained. Inductive statistics via the application of probability theory supply several hypothetical distributions of this type. These distributions present the probability of the occurrence of a given outcome by chance upon the application of a prediction. The given prediction is phrased in the negative (the null hypothesis) so that the hypothetical distribution is actually a distribution of the expected number of times a prediction will not apply.

Therefore, a sociologist using inductive statistics proceeds in the following way. He tests his prediction by applying its negative to the events it designates. He compares the outcome with the chance distribution of probable outcomes supplied by probability theory. He uses certain statistical techniques to compare the obtained outcome with the predicted outcome. He then decides whether or not to reject his prediction: whether or not it does not apply. Inductive statistics, then, provide a way of circumventing the arduous task of repeatedly applying a prediction to the events in its domain. The sociologist need only apply his prediction once and then compare it to the hypothetical distribution.

But what superficially appears to be a blessing is actually a burden. At the same time that inductive statistics circumvent the repeated application of a prediction to its domain, they also dispose of the necessary technique for decreasing predictive error in theory. In this sense, use of inductive statistics maintains the low level of precision of sociological predictions.

CLASS 2 PHENOMENA AND INDUCTIVE STATISTICS

Survey research relies heavily on inductive statistics because of the difficulties and complexities involved in using large numbers of questionnaries or interviews and analyzing the results. Predictions to be tested by this method, therefore, are usually applied only once to events in their domain: survey research is generally not replicated. Hence the use of inductive statistics is necessary. Furthermore, survey research is the methodology employed to study class 2 phenomena. Given this interdependency, it follows that class 2 phenomena and survey research with its heavy use of inductive statistics tend to maintain the low level of precision in sociological theory and, concomitantly, to maintain the high levels of predictive error because they circumvent one of the necessary techniques for reducing predictive error.

CLASS 2 PHENOMENA RECONSIDERED

The study of class 2 phenomena by the majority of sociologists, then, generates two sets of deleterious interdependencies. First, reports about human behavior tend to be expressed in group terminology. Group terminology tends to succumb to the language and definitional problems previously discussed. These problems in turn lead to high levels of error in sociological predictions and thus to low levels of precision in sociological theory. Second, survey research is the methodology employed to study reports about human behavior. This methodology tends to be a one-shot affair and of necessity relies heavily on inductive statistics. The use of inductive statistics is a method for circumventing replication, or the repeated application of predictions to the empirical events they predict. Replication is a necessary technique for reducing the magnitude of these language problems and hence for reducing predictive error. Therefore, the study of class 2 phenomena via survey research tends to maintain the low levels of precision in sociological theory.

CONCLUSION

Survey research and the study of class 2 phenomena need not be as problematic as they are for sociology. The use of replication, logical and semantic rigor, and systematic study of the relationships between reports about human behavior and the observable human behavior these reports designate would suffice to solve the problems. But this is a large order that counters the ingrained tendencies of sociologists. These solutions are not immediately forthcoming. In fact, the problems are not even generally known.

Summary

It is commonplace in the philosophy of science to distinguish between a theory language and an object language as the major components of any theory. This distinction is heuristic at best. Sociologists have reified it so as to justify their tendency to maintain a schism between their theory construction endeavors and their empirical research. This schism is counter to all the lessons of the history of science. Sociologists also tend to misuse their primitive terms: terms that are assumed to designate directly observable events do not actually do so.

They study either observable human behavior itself via observation or experimentation or reports about observable human behavior via questionnaires and interviews. The study of these reports (class 2 phenomena) requires intensive research into the relationship between reports and the behavior they describe, but this research has not been conducted in sociology. This class of phenomena implies the use of group terminology. The terminology consists of summarizing, summating, and *sui generis* terms, which are all subject to the language problems mentioned in the last chapter. When these terms are vague and are used in predictions, the amount of logico-deductive error is inestimable. When they are ambiguous and are used in predictions it is estimable. When they are opaque and contradictory there is no truth value in the predictions.

Disposition concepts and definitions are necessary to designate human behavior. If the perceptual reality sociology should study is human behavior, then sociologists should use disposition concepts and definitions. However, these are rarely used in sociology. Sociologists also lack an adequate set of terms to designate verbal behavior, social change, and physiological variables. They are satisfied with positing the least precise predictions: statistical predictions that do not allow for the estimation of predictive error. Finally, those who study reports about human behavior rely heavily on inductive statistics, which provide a technique for bypassing the arduous replication of research. However, such replication is a necessary means of diminishing predictive error. Thus, the study of reports about human behavior implies large amounts of predictive error.

[FOUR]

Systematization, Explication, and the Appeal to Observables: Partial Solutions

THREE TRENDS have become prominent in sociology for dealing with the imprecision of its language system: systematization, explication, and dealing with observable human behavior. What is the efficacy of each of these?

Systematization

We defined systematization as the rearranging of one's theoretical terms so as to maximize the contributing effects of such relational factors as grammar and contextual meaning to a general increase in the level of precision of one's language system. Two present trends in sociology are subsets of this technique: axiomatization and mathematical model building. We can first consider Hans Zetterberg's (1954; 1965) original proposal for the axiomatization of sociological theory, and then turn to Blalock's (1964; 1968; 1969) important contributions with respect to the application of mathematical causal models to sociological theory building.

Sociological Axiomatization

Professor Zetterberg's stated program involves the formulation of deductive-axiomatic theories. At the highest level of generality in these theories would be a limited number of axioms and postulates from which would be deduced a larger number of theorems that would specify testable relations between empirical (social) events. Although he consistently refers to issues relevant to nonexperimental, survey-type sociological research, these theorems would presumably be testable in terms of experimental sociological research as well. The point is that he is advocating axiomatic theory building as a general approach for all sociologists.

The first necessary and sufficient step is for the sociologist to state explicitly the basic concepts or primitive terms, that may go undefined in his theoretical language system. Using these primitive terms, the sociologist then defines his derived concepts or terms. The specific definitional form advocated is nominal definition. These nominally defined, derived concepts are then used in formulating the postulates and hypotheses of axiomatic sociological theory. Corresponding to each nominal definition is an operational definition. These operational definitions are used in formulating the testable theorems that are deduced from the original postulates. At this stage, the sociologist is free to test his theorems, thereby indirectly testing the efficacy of his axiomatic theory.

Zetterberg (1954: 22–25) gives as an example an axiomatized version of a theory of the division of labor that is "a distorted version of Durkheim's theory of division of labor" in a society. He first assumes that the sociological researcher has studied a number of groups with respect to "six variables" and has found these variables to be interrelated in certain ways. Furthermore, he assumes that these interrelationships among the six variables (they need not concern us) are expressed in terms of fourteen theorems that have been subjected to validating empirical tests. For example, the following are the first three theorems he presents:

The greater the division of labor, the more the uniformity.
The greater the solidarity, the greater the number of members.
The greater the number of members, the less the deviation.

He then sets about "summarizing these findings according to the model of the axiomatic theory." He introduces the following basic concepts:

behavior	solidarity
member	division of labor
group	rejection
norm	

He formulates the following as derived concepts nominally defined:

uniformity: the proportion of members whose behavior is the norm of the group.
deviation: the proportion of members whose behavior is not the norm of the group.
deviate: member whose behavior is not the norm of the group.

Finally, he selects four postulates from which "all fourteen findings can be derived as they are combined with each other and with the nominal definitions." The following example will suffice to give the general form of these postulates:

The greater the division of labor, the greater the solidarity.

Further on in the book Zetterberg considers the relationship between nominal definitions and operational definitions in more detail. Operational definitions are used "to interpret the nominal definitions of our hypothesis into terms more acceptable for research." Although there is some confusion here because of the interchangeability of his use of the terms "hypothesis" and "postulate," it is apparent that he considers the utility of operational definitions to be the degree to which they are used to formulate empirical tests of the theorems or hypotheses at the deductive base of a particular sociological axiomatized theory. He offers the following examples (1954: 30):

Nominal definition: the degree of division of labor in a society.
Operational definition: the number of occupations in a society.
Nominal definition: the degree of rejection of deviates from society norms.
Operational definition: the proportion of laws demanding death penalty, deportation or long prison terms.

In a subsequent chapter he turns to a consideration of the possible ways in which nominal definition and operational definition may fail to correspond in a one-to-one relation with each other. He labels such lack of exact correspondence as problems of "validity."

Zetterberg claims that several distinct advantages accrue from the axiomatization of sociological theory. By and large, these advantages are *genuine*, and I will not make explicit reference to them. Furthermore, Costner and Leik (1964) point out a serious discrepancy in Zetterberg's claims that certain hypotheses can be deduced or derived from certain postulates. This criticism is sound and will not concern us further. What I want to emphasize is that as beneficial and/or as faulty as certain aspects of the axiomatization of sociological theory may be, it is at best a partial solution to the definitional-theoretical problems of sociology we have seen.

ONLY A PARTIAL SOLUTION

First of all, in Zetterberg's example he is assuming the validation of certain empirical relations between certain empirical entities. He lists the terms designating these empirical entities as his basic concepts. And these basic concepts are members of the traditional core terminology of sociology. In effect, therefore, he is assuming that these particular core terms have a high level of precision of usage, since any attempt at axiomatization that is used to systematize the relations between pre-existing sociological terms must of necessity assume their legitimacy and precision. Another way of saying this is that since systematization is a control technique applied to a pre-existing language system, any particular instance of systematization, like axiomatization, must accept certain terms as given and therefore (implicitly) as highly precise. This assumption is quite problematic for sociology because of the low level of precision in its core terms and the pervasiveness of its language problems. Zetterberg's choice of basic concepts clearly reveals this. Such core sociological terms as "group," "norm," "solidarity," and "rejection" cannot be legitimately treated as basic concepts or primitive terms because of their vagueness, ambiguity, and possible contradiction and opacity in usage. It is simply unjustified to assume that they are sufficiently precise or that there is a high level of agreement among sociologists as to their semantic and grammatical usage. Furthermore, given this imprecision, it is quite certain that they will have a low yield in empirical utility and theoretical fertility. And this leads into a second reason why this assumption is problematic.

Zetterberg in particular, but also sociologists in general confuse their levels of analysis. So, with the above example Zetterberg uses some core terms as primitives in the sense that they designate directly observable empirical entities. But such terms as "norm" and "solidarity" do not. They must be further specified by the use of unconditional and conditional object predicates in definitional chains of varying complexity before they can be made to designate observable, discriminable empirical entities. Moreover, since these terms have not yet been defined, they obviously cannot be used in hypotheses or theorems assumed to designate relations between directly observable events.

Theoretical statements that are assigned the lowest positions at the deductive base in axiomatized sociological theories are often more appropriately considered postulates or propositions of high generality. This is clearly the case in Zetterberg's example. Consider the following "hypothesis" or theorem, for example: "The greater the division of labor, the more the uniformity." This hypothesis is better conceived of as a higher-order postulate in any axiomatized sociological theory that uses it. Zetterberg, himself, seems to realize this when further on in his discussion he admits an operational definition of "the division of labor" into his theoretical language system. But if he realizes this, he does so without explicitly stating the problem and while implicitly oversimplifying it. It is doubtful whether one simple operational definition of "the division of labor" would suffice to delimit the total meaning of the term. One can conceive of multiple operational definitions of the term, as well as multiple dispositional definitions intervening between the term "the division of labor" and any directly observable empirical event that is designated by any limited number of its member defining predicates. Given these multiple specifying definitions forming complex definitional chains, it follows that this hypothesis is in actuality a higher-order postulate from which multiple testable theorems can (possibly) be deduced. Zetterberg is therefore impeding both the empirical utility and the theoretical fertility of the use of this term by his unfortunately naïve and oversimplified theoretical statement. The same criticism can be lodged against the term "uniformity" in the above "hypothesis."

ON THE CAUSES OF THE TRANSPOSITION PROBLEM

This transposition of hypotheses and postulates in sociological axiomatized theories is partially the result of confusion among sociologists about the appropriate status of primitives in such theoretical systems. This confusion is the result, in turn, of a lack of both an adequate set of simple primitives and a theoretically fertile and empirically useful set of abstract primitives. This is to say, because sociological terminology lacks both types of primitives, any effort at axiomatization must be preceded by the development of such primitives. In this sense, this type of systematization is still premature in sociological theory. The axiomatized theories that have been formed are at best no more than illustrations of a technique.

ZETTERBERG'S USE OF DEFINITION

Zetterberg's rules of correspondence between nominal and operational definitions are oversimplications of what must be a quite complicated set of definitional chains, given the complexity of the empirical phenomena that are to be specified at the terminal stage of definition. Whereas he has an operational definition in juxtaposition with a nominal definition, in actuality such nominal definitions must themselves be specified by definitional chains that make use of conditional and unconditional object predicates that are directly empirically accessible. His nominal definition of "deviate" provides a good example: "deviate: member whose behavior is not the norm of the group." What constitutes a "group" must first be explained and this is a highly complex task:

1. A group is two or more people in proximity in time and space who are interacting.

2. People are in proximity if they are within speaking distance of each other (usually two to five feet apart).

3. People are in proximity if they are within speaking distance of each other at $T_1 \ldots {}_n$

4. People are interacting with each other if any given individual is the recipient of stimuli emitted from all the other members of the group, severally or together, between T_1 and T_{1+n}, and if this individual elicits responses from any or all other members of the group, severally or together, between T_1 and T_{1+n}

5. The above conditions for interaction can be further specified as follows. . . .

Of course, this definitional chain can be extended greatly, but it must terminate at some finite point. Where this point shall be is determined by the explicit needs of the researcher, which in turn result from his exact theoretical objectives. But "group" must be defined further through many intervening steps before it can be employed in an operational definition. And the same is true of "norm" and "behavior." For example, consider the needed specification of norm:

1. A norm is a finite set of behaviors that the members of a group agree are necessary and sufficient for an individual to perform in order to be considered a member of the group.

2. It is necessary that the members of the group be able to describe these behaviors.

3. It is necessary that the members of the group be able to agree on a given set of descriptions.

4. It is necessary that the members of the group be able to agree on whether or not a given member has performed these behaviors.

5. It is necessary that the behaviors and the relative performance of these behaviors by any one member be discriminable and observable to the other members of the group.

6. By "members" of the group is meant a simple majority of the group members . . . (etc.)

And, of course, it is equally true with this definitional chain that the particular researcher may extend it or terminate it at whatever point he feels is sufficient for his purposes. But he must define "norm" before it can be used in an operational definition.

Two more criticisms can be made of Zetterberg's use of definition in the framework of the axiomatization of sociological theory. First of all, his ubiquitous use of nominal definition overlooks the previously mentioned bad effects such definition can have on the level of precision of any theoretical language system, especially sociological theory language. Second, the operational definitions he provides by way of example are insufficient as operational definitions. Consider the following examples:

Nominal definition: the degree of division of labor in a society.
Operational definition: the number of occupations in a society.

These proposed operational definitions are in actuality composites of multiple concealed definitions. What categorization of occupations is the researcher going to use? What is a society? What are the boundaries of a given society? How are these boundaries to be assessed? Zetterberg has labeled as an operational definition a complex predicate whose component terms are too vague to be components of an operational definition.

ZETTERBERG'S PREDICTIVE STATEMENTS

All the cited examples of Zetterberg's predictions demonstrate his satisfaction with predictions at the lowest level of precision. He makes no effort even to include an error term, let alone estimating its possible magnitude. True, his predictions are an initial attempt at systematization, and empirical application of these predictions would seem premature. However, estimation of the magnitude of the error is possible conceptually by positing all those reasonable conditions under which one would not expect the predictions to hold. This dialectic method is a reasoning procedure that has proved fruitful in other sciences. Furthermore, his book has been available for twenty years and in that time there have apparently been no attempts to estimate error in these predictions. Finally, his uncritical use of group terminology guarantees a continued low level of precision in his predictions.

SUMMARY

In effect, Zetterberg is using a language precision control device and at the same time making certain assumptions and engaging in certain practices that reduce the benefits such a device is supposed to confer. This was true of his unequivocal acceptance of the theoretical language system of sociology as highly precise, of his transposition of levels of analysis so that nonprimitive terms were used inappropriately as simple primitive terms and postulates were confused with theorems, of his overextended use of nominal definition and his misconceived correspondence rules concerning nominal and operational definitions, and finally, of his satisfaction with statistical predictions and group terminologies of the lowest level of precision. Moreover, it should be noted that he also places great emphasis upon statistical, inferential techniques as evaluational devices, thereby reneging on the scientific prerequisite of direct and systematic replication of tests of hypotheses (see Chapter 3). Be that as it may, the important point to be gleaned from all this is that Zetterberg is proposing a sophisticated systematization device for sociology but at the same time repeating many of the definitional-theoretical difficulties sociology is subject to (for a more contemporary example see Blau, 1970 and Gross, 1959). It is in this important sense that systematization is at best a partial answer for these problems in sociology.

Mathematical Model Building in Sociology

The work of Hubert M. Blalock is in the foreground with respect to the application of mathematics to sociological theory building. His book, *Causal Inferences in Nonexperimental Research* (1964) is a succinct statement of the arguments employed in this approach.* I am not

---

* This presentation of Blalock's (and others') work in this area is, of course, brief and does not do justice to his ingenuity. I am assuming that a certain amount of knowledge is possessed by the reader and have presented this brief sketch just to delineate the general area of concern.

attempting a critique of the work of one man, except as it exemplifies a general trend among sociologists who are concerned with doing something about the low level of precision in their theoretical language system.

Blalock advocates the construction of "causal models." This involves the specific statement of cause-and-effect relations between selected "variables" or terms signifying "variables." Causal diagrams are used to specify these relations, with a "⟶" between any two terms indicating a cause-and-effect relationship. So that if "status inconsistency" is said to cause "psychosomatic symptoms," the appropriate causal diagram would be:

Status inconsistency ⟶ psychosomatic symptoms

The next step in the development of causal models is to substitute letter symbols for the terms in the diagrams. So that if we let "status inconsistency" be designated by X and "psychosomatic symptoms" be designated by Y, the above causal diagram becomes:

$$X \longrightarrow Y$$

The final step is to formulate a set of equations that will sufficiently describe the causal diagrams. The above causal model could be described by the following equation.

$$X = Y + e_1$$

The e_1 is the amount of error in the causal relationship that is due to possible outside influences on the Y. In effect, the e_1 term is the margin of error that is to be expected in this causal prediction.*

Although many types of equations can be utilized to describe the many types of causal relations between various sociological variables,

* These types of predictions have a disputed logical status. As McFarland (1970) notes, "cause" is so vague as to make a precise interpretation of "A causes B" impossible. Without this interpretation no rules of deduction can be specified. Despite this difficulty, I will use Blalock's terminology.

Blalock concentrates here on what he calls "recursive systems." * The description of these types of equation sets should suffice to convey the general idea of what is involved in mathematical causal model building in sociology. The following is a recursive causal diagram:

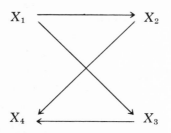

This diagram may be described by the following set of equations:

$$X_1 = e_1$$

$$X_2 = b_{21}X_1 + e_2$$

$$X_3 = b_{31}X_1 + b_{32}X_2 + e_3$$

$$X_4 = b_{41}X_1 + b_{42}X_2 + b_{43}X_3 + e_4$$

Each X symbol used in this set of equations stands for a term designating a sociological variable. Again, the e terms designate the margin of error in any causal prediction that is represented in the diagram. This recursive system rules out two-way causation or feedback causal relations between the variables. It is also assumed that the causal relations are best described by additive relationships between the variables and that the e terms are not correlated with each other or with any of the independent variables (signified by the X symbols on the right-hand side of any single equation). For my purposes, these assumptions need not be dealt with in detail.

The b terms signify the regression coefficients that describe the relation between the dependent variable and any one independent variable:

---

* It should be noted that Blalock and other sociologists are now engaged in formulating more complicated mathematical models involving simultaneous differential equations to describe change and feedback relations between sociological variables (see Blalock, 1969).

b_{21}, for example, signifies the regression of X_1 on X_2, X_1 being the independent variable and X_2 the dependent variable. The types of causal predications one can make from such models involve the disappearance of certain designated partial correlations or regression slopes. (Blalock advocates emphasis on regression coefficients rather than correlation coefficients.) Hence, "the prediction equations can therefore be written in the form of some partial correlation [or regression slope] set equal to 'zero.'" (p. 64) The details of this need not detain us; a simple example will suffice. If one assumes away a direct causal link between X_1 and X_3 in the above causal diagram, the partial correlation $r_{13:2}$ (the correlation between X_1 and X_3 controlling for X_2) would equal zero, and the partial slope $b_{31:2}$ (the regression between X_1 and X_3 controlling for X_2) would also equal zero. Or one may assume away the causal relations between X_1 and X_4, X_1 and X_3, and X_2 and X_4, leaving the following causal diagram:

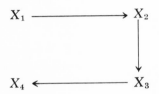

In this case the prediction equations would be: $r_{13:2} = 0$, $r_{14:23} = 0$, and $r_{24:13} = 0$. The general idea, then, is that one first assumes a given causal model and then derives predictions about the (partial) correlations and (partial) regressions by making alterations in the original model, so that these predictions will take the form of setting the (partial) correlation and regression coefficients equal to zero. Then one goes about testing these predictions by collecting relevant data and computing the necessary correlation and regression coefficients to see if within certain preassessed limits of error the derived predictions are true: i.e., the given partials are at zero or close enough to zero to justify saying they are zero.

THE ADVANTAGES OF MATHEMATICAL MODEL BUILDING

One advantage of this approach to sociological theory building is that, within the limitations of present theory, it permits the formulation of causal models and causal predictions based on these models. This is to say that it attempts to systematize the relations between given sociological terms (variables), thereby working toward an increase in the level of precision of the whole sociological language system. A second advantage that has the same effect is the introduction of mathematics into sociological theory. As is continually emphasized by the philosophers of science, mathematics is a language system with high precision (see Kemeny, 1959). It makes full use of the control devices mentioned in previous chapters in order to restrict the general language problems also mentioned in previous chapters; it implements a vigorous system of logic and definition formation in order to cope with semantic, contextual, and grammatical ambiguity, vagueness, opacity (in a limited sense), and contradiction. By establishing equivalence relations between mathematical language and sociological language, the former with all of its precision (presumably) becomes substitutible for the latter with all of its imprecision.

THE RECOGNIZED DISADVANTAGES OF THIS APPROACH

As Blalock points out, however, one pays a price for these gains by making certain assumptions that are necessitated by the inductive (statistical) form of the argument. Aside from the specific assumptions necessitated by the use of recursive systems in particular (e.g., additivity), certain general assumptions in this approach limit its utility for increasing the precision of sociological theoretical language. These assumptions derive from the very limitations of sociological theory.

Among these limitations Blalock notes the following: "substantial measurement errors, the inability to randomize and replicate, a high percentage of unexplained variation, and numerous unmeasured variables and unclear concepts" (p. viii). And he is clear that his proposed solution is not a real solution: he invokes certain assumptions that in effect deny limitations. For example, with respect to the high level of error (for whatever reason) in sociological predictions, he states that "at some point one must stop [the infinite regress in search for possible confounding causal factors] and make the simplifying assumption that variables left out do not produce confounding influences." (p. 176) Other relevant considerations that make this only a partial solution to the definitional-theoretical problems of sociology go unmentioned. These omissions are similar to Zetterberg's.

First of all, high precision in the core terminology of sociological language is assumed. Symbols are used to designate sociological terms or variables: e.g., X = status inconsistency. This, in effect, assumes a constancy and accuracy of meaning that these terms just do not possess. Since the symbols stay constant and reliable from context to context and are freely substituted for the terms they designate, one is led to the conclusion that these terms have the reliability and validity of the symbols.

Consider the relation between the symbol and the term as a defining relation, so that the above example is equivalent to saying, "Status inconsistency is X." This definition is sufficient as an illustration of what a definition is, but it is clearly insufficient to introduce "status inconsistency" into a theoretical language system as a highly precise term. And this is what is being done. The symbol X stands as the unspecified defining predicate of "status inconsistency" and is presumed to be its complete definition. It can therefore be substituted for status inconsistency in causal models or sets of mathematical causal statements. But because X is unspecified, this definition is, on the one hand, at the lowest level of precision, and on the other, not a true definition at all.

Now this free substitution of symbols for one's terms is legitimate if the symbols designate a set or subset of highly precise defining object predicates (of whatever form) rather than the term they define. In other words, if "status inconsistency" were defined thus: "Status inconsistency is A, B, and C," A, B, and C were sets of highly precise object predicates (presumably both conditional and unconditional), and X was substituted for A, B, and C, then the free use of X as a substitute for "status inconsistency" would be perfectly legitimate. Of course, if this definition were complete then this is equivalent to substituting X for "status inconsistency" because

Status inconsistency is A, B, and C.
$X = A$, B, and C.
X = status inconsistency.

On the other hand, if this definition is incomplete no such equivalence pertains because

> Status inconsistency is A, B, C, D, and E.
> $X = A$, B, and C; but not D and E.
> $X =$ status inconsistency.
> $X =$ part of the total meaning of status inconsistency.

The latter condition will probably be the one most often pertinent to sociological terms. This will result in the formation of mathematical causal models of a lower order of generality than those presumed by Blalock (and others in this field of endeavor). In other words, such causal statements as "status inconsistency→psychosomatic symptoms" will in actuality be higher-order propositions or axioms, and causal models will be at the level of devices to test lower-order propositions or postulates and theorems derived from these axioms.

I mention this not so much as a criticism of causal model building, but as an aside that illustrates one possible inaccurate interpretation of the proper functioning of causal models resulting from this assumed free substitutivity of mathematical symbols and core sociological terms. Such substitution is quite illegitimate, given the language problems of most core sociological terms. Even at the level of lower theoretical generality (i.e., postulates and theorems) the utility of mathematical causal models is open to question in sociology. Sociologists have not yet attained sufficient definitional accuracy to incompletely define their core terms; so how could they make profitable use of the less general type of causal model building that is possible when symbols can be substituted for incomplete definitions? Construction of a precise theoretical language is a prerequisite to making causal statements of any level of generality which use the component terms of that language. The overall effect of the free use of symbols and mathematical language in sociology is to legitimate an imprecise theory language.

This point is crucial and cannot be overemphasized. Another way of making it is to examine a specific causal model offered by Blalock (1967a: 101–108) elsewhere, but one that still derives from his orientation. Consider the following causal model, which has to do with minority group relations:

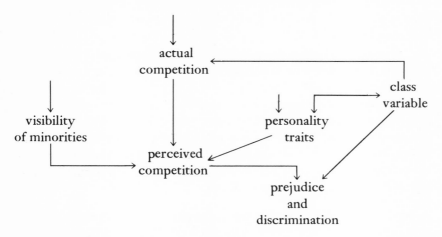

Various indicators could be and are given for the component terms of this causal model: e.g., "personality traits" are measured by the use of various questionnaires that are supposed to reveal the presence of certain traits, upon differential responding to different items by specific subjects. Even if these indicators are considered to be valid and reliable, they are at best incomplete definitions of rather abstract terms. It is obvious that terms like these have a great deal of vagueness (and possibly opacity, ambiguity, and contradiction as well, depending on their usage). This vagueness results in the measurement errors, the high percentage of unexplained variation, and the unclear concepts that Blalock mentions. For example, "competition" is never defined by reference to observable, empirical events either directly or indirectly by definitional chains. Insofar as this term is predicated on human behavioral referents, it must be so defined to attain precision of usage. It follows that the phenomena designated by this term cannot possibly be accurately measured (with a tolerably low margin of error) until the term is defined by reference to empirical phenomena that are observable. So this example leads us to the same conclusion: mathematical model building in sociology should be preceded by or used in conjunction with the formation of a precise core terminology based on precise definition and observation. Without the fulfillment of this basic prerequisite, such model building will have a low yield of empirical utility and theoretical fertility.

THE PROBLEM OF SYMBOL SUBSTITUTION: AN ANALOGY

To a theoretician one of the most stimulating of events is the confirmation of his statements or arguments by statements or arguments made by others with entirely different concerns. Having a cursory interest in nuclear physics I decided to delve deeper into the theory of relativity and I encountered the following arguments by Herbert Dingle (1965) against the primary emphasis on mathematical models by nuclear physicists. My basic argument against mathematical model building in sociology is analogous to his argument against mathematical model building (my term, not his) in nuclear physics.

But the effect of the relativity theory on philosophy has been to concentrate attention on the instruments used to represent experiences by concepts—in particular, language—as though they were the ultimate objects of philosophical thought. This is the counterpart of the situation in science, in which mathematics is in the saddle and rides physics . . . The only difference is that while the linguistic philosophers allow their symbols to say nothing, the mathematicians make theirs talk nonsense. This is not to decry the study of languages—it is a necessary study—but when we allow it to release us from the duty of saying something until we have solved all the problems they present, which in all likelihood we shall never do, we go badly astray. . . .

Physical considerations now count for nothing; the mathematics is all. If a symbol is given the letter s, then our experiences of time must necessarily follow the course that the symbol takes in the logically impeccable theory. [p. xii]

GROUP TERMINOLOGY, STATISTICS, PREDICTIVE ERROR

Blalock's approach assumes the sufficiency of group terminology; hence the magnitude of predictive error will always tend to be large. Moreover, it makes extensive use of inductive statistics and thus contributes to the tendency not to replicate; the level of predictive error will therefore tend to remain high. It deals exclusively with class 2 phenomena, and because of that domain, reinforces and contributes to the circle of events that keeps sociological predictions at low levels of precision. Finally, estimation of predictive error under this system is at best open-ended and at worst purely symbolic.

SUMMARY AND CONCLUSIONS

Many of the criticisms made of Zetterberg apply equally to Blalock. These criticisms derive from common assumptions and omissions that both make within their respective conceptual frameworks. Similarities between them should be apparent: the assumption that sociological core terminology is sufficiently precise to be accepted as an essentially nonproblematic given, the confusion of abstract primitives with simple primitives, the statistical form of the predictions accepted or formulated, the use of group terminology, the use of inductive statistics, and the general research strategy that is implied. With respect to the latter, I would like to emphasize one especially important point. I have heard several sociologists, influenced by Blalock's work as well as the new methodological fervor in the field, maintain that one can make any theoretical assumptions he wants as long as he explicitly lists those assumptions he does make. This type of argument is invalid for reasons similar to those that made the extreme nominalist position invalid. The situation is not as relativistic as this argument would have it. *Sociologists can make any theoretical assumptions they want, provided that these assumptions do not result in consequences precluding a method of inquiry that will increase the level of precision in their theory language.* Sociologists are bound by whatever restrictions that can be applied to their discipline which will increase the level of precision of their theories. Assumptions that negate any of these restrictions or that work counter to them are not justifiable. In both Zetterberg's and Blalock's work such assumptions were made, thereby restricting the utility of these forms of systematization in sociological theory.

Explication

THE CASE FOR A MORE PRECISE SOCIOLOGICAL TERMINOLOGY

Dumont and Wilson (1967) have set forth "explication" as a particular solution to the language problems of sociological terminology. They certify it as a "program" whereby certain "key isolated abstract concepts in sociology" can be made more precise. Before certain of their proposals are examined in detail, and "explication" is discussed as a technique mentioned extensively in the literature on the philosophy of science, two points should be made clear. First, explication as such is not a novel or peculiar control technique to increase the precision of one's language usage. It is a special case of explicit definition: "special" because it involves the *re*definition of terms that are already in use in a given language system. Second, as Dumont and Wilson point out, "explication" is a vague term in and of itself. They fail to note however, exactly how vague a term it is. The exact specification of the criteria for a "*sufficiently* explicated term" varies considerably among the advocates of explication. Both of these points will be made clearer in what follows.

DEFINING "EXPLICATION"

Hempel offers the following definition of "explication": "Explication is concerned with expressions whose meaning in conversational language or even in scientific discourse is more or less vague and aims at giving those expressions a new and precisely determined meaning . . ." (1952: 11). He goes on to specify "meaning analysis and empirical analysis" as the two components of explication. Meaning analysis focuses on the meanings of linguistic expressions. It makes terms already in use explicit by providing synonymous expressions which have to be previously understood. Empirical analysis "states characteristics which are as a matter of empirical fact, both necessary and sufficient for the empirical realization of the phenomenon under analysis" (p. 10). Hempel goes on to state that for any given instance of explication to be necessary and sufficient it must fulfill two basic requirements:

1. [The explicated concepts] must permit the reformulation in syntactically precise sentences of a large part of what is customarily expressed by them.

2. [The explicated concepts] must permit the development of a comprehensive, rigorous and sound theoretical system. [p. 11]

Hempel's is only one conceptualization of explication, but it is the one upon which Dumont and Wilson build their argument for explication of certain sociological concepts. Hanna (1968) provides a good survey of the literature on this term. Much of the vagueness associated with explication, according to him, results from variation in the strictness of the substitutivity requirement for the term that is explicated (explicandum) and the set of predicates used to explicate it (explication).

At one extreme are those who permit the explication and explicandum to be unrelated in meaning. This is analogous to the general definitional requirement of eliminability, which demands that the defining predicates be understandable independently of the defined term. At the other extreme are those who stipulate that the explication and explicandum be synonymous. This is analogous to the general definitional requirement of substitutivity, which demands that the defining predicates be equivalent in meaning to the defined term. Hanna rejects both extremes and favors equivalence between the extensions of the explication and explicandum as the necessary and sufficient condition for adequate use of explication. By this he means that the set of empirical phenomena that is designated by the empirically accessible object predicates forming the explication should be equivalent to the set of empirical phenomena that is designated by the empirically accessible object predicates, specified or specifiable, which are the original components of the explicandum. The latter object predicates are usually specifiable, thereby making the original term quite vague. Equivalence of extension as the requirement for adequate explication can thus be interpreted as specification of the specifiable object predicates, either by making them explicit or by providing a different set of specified object predicates that designate the same phenomena as the original specifiable object predicates. In either case explication is still just a special case of explicit definition.

Although Hanna finally settles on this requirement of the equivalence of extensions as the necessary and sufficient condition for precise explication, he also notes the possibility of explicating the intension of a particular term. He calls this "explication $_1$" as opposed to the explication of a term's extension, which is "explication $_2$." The former is equivalent to Hempel's requirement that the explicated terms "permit the reformulation in syntactically precise sentences of a large part of what is customarily expressed by them [the explicated terms]." Both of these types of explication refer to the necessity for an explicated term to permit a high level of precision in syntactic usage and contextual meaning. This is to say that the explicated term must not only match the level of grammatical and contextual meaning precision that it had prior to being explicated, but that it must also exceed this previous level of precision. And herein is the most obvious convergence between explication and systematization as language precision control devices. To the extent that the grammatical and contextual relations between a given term and other terms are being systematized, the intension of that term is being explicated. In other words, if one is focusing on systematizing a particular term, he is explicating the grammatical and contextual meaning of that term.

In their application of explication to the problems of sociological terminology, Dumont and Wilson alter its general meaning for their specific purposes. They define it in accordance with Hempel's definition: explication is "the process whereby an initially vague and imprecise concept may be attributed with a more exact meaning, thereby increasing the likelihood of its intersubjective certifiability" (1967: 990). The criterion of "intersubjective certifiability" is defined after Hempel: "the terms used in formulating scientific statements should have clearly specified meanings and be understood in the same sense by all who use them" (1967: 989). They also specify "meaning analysis" and "empirical analysis" as the two components of explication. But in defining these they are addressing themselves specifically to the explication of sociological terms; "the first procedural step of meaning analysis involves a survey of the literature in an attempt to cull out the most basic implicit or explicit assumptions inherent in the various meanings that have been attributed to the concept" (p. 991). What they call assumptions are predicative statements with abstract (in the sense of not directly empirically accessible) object predicates. For example, when they explicate "social status" (p. 994) they isolate two complex predicates: that observers can perceive and discriminate an attribute or set of attributes that are assigned to individuals, and that an observer or observers can "order others meaningfully in terms of this attribute." So an "assumption" in their sense is a predicative statement in which a particular nominal (sociological term) stands in an identity relation with a particular predicate (of varying forms). Such assumptions form the meaning of the term. The first step in meaning analysis of a particular sociological term is collecting and making explicit all such assumptions (predicative statements) in which the particular term has been used by previous theorists. In accordance with the terminology used at the start of the book, Dumont and Wilson are suggesting that the first step in explicating a sociological term is to convert its vagueness into ambiguity.

The second phase of meaning analysis "involves certain decisions concerning the syntactic status of the concepts defining phrases" (p. 992). Here they are referring to the necessity for making explicit the grammatical and contextual meaning of the particular term. Although their examples are confusing here ("Is the concept a class of property term . . . Or is it customary to conceive of it as a comparative term" [p. 992]), they seem to be saying that this step in meaning analysis can be accomplished by specifying how the term has been used in grammatical and semantic context. This, of course, can be accomplished through the use of conditional object predicates that specify the linguistic functioning of the particular term with respect to other terms.

"Empirical analysis" involves ascertaining the empirical existence and observability of the phenomena designated by the empirically accessible object predicates that make up the sociological term's referential meaning. Or, as they phrase it, "the empirical analysis of a concept refers to that process whereby the basic assumptions which have been brought to light as a result of the meaning analysis are submitted to direct empirical test" (p. 992). Whatever the phraseology, they are saying that empirical analysis involves the assessment of the observability of the designated sociological objects, properties, or relations. The term "empirical test" is somewhat misleading in this definition. "Measurement" would have been a more appropriate term—insofar as measurement is a process whereby empirical phenomena designated by certain object predicates are made directly observable at high levels of precision. Their example of the empirical analysis of social status should suffice to illustrate this:

. . . an empirical analysis of 'social status' should seek to provide at least a tentative answer to the following question: does there exist a measurable attribute, social status, such that a single individual and/or a number of individuals can order others meaningfully on terms of this attribute. [p. 994]

Thus, an empirical analysis of "social status" would involve "measuring" the object predicates that have been specified by the meaning analysis of the term: i.e., assuring that these object predicates designated observable empirical phenomena. It is an interesting aside that the term "meaningfully" in the above example is critical to understanding this statement, but it is not sufficiently specified. The situation is clarified if the statement is given this possibly equivalent interpretation: *An empirical analysis of "social status" should seek to provide at least a tentative answer to the following question: are the empirical phenomena designated by the defining object predicates of "social status" observable or measurable, and if they are, can the term so defined be used in empirically useful and theoretically fertile predictions about social behavior?*

THE SHORTCOMINGS OF EXPLICATION

As I have mentioned earlier, there is no such thing as a complete description. The terminal stage of any definitional chain will be determined by the degree to which such a stage in definition is assessed to permit the formation of empirically useful predictive statements with tolerable margins of error. This same criterion applies to the termination of explication. Any given instance of explication will almost necessarily involve the use of definitional chains of varying complexity. This will invariably be true of the explication of sociological terms. Predicates that will be used to explicate a given sociological term will themselves have to be explicated, and the predicates used in this explication will have to be explicated, and so on. The terminal stage of explication of a given sociological term will occur when the explicated terms become components of empirically useful hypotheses and theorems having to do with social phenomena. Given the present lack of such hypotheses and theorems in sociology, the terminal stage of explication thus becomes problematic. This type of interdependency between definitions and theoretical predictive statements in sociology (and in general) has important ramifications for the deductive assumption involved in explication, which I shall shortly consider in detail.

THE PROBLEM OF RESIDUE OF MEANING

Any attempt at explicating any particular sociological term will have to come to grips with the large connotative component of the term. This means that one must specify the exact semantic status of that part of the term's meaning (usually its connotative aspect) that is not to be included in the explicated meaning of the term. If this is not done, this residue of meaning will tend to hamper the acquisition of high levels of semantic agreement among sociologists using the term. Every time sociologists debate the proper definition of a term, they implicitly recognize the problem.

Be that as it may, how can a sociological theorist specify the exact semantic status of the residue of meaning in the terms he explicates? By way of answering this question, it should be pointed out that both the above problems with explication in sociology are related to the overall issue of ascertaining when a particular definition is complete and when it is incomplete. The first problem, explicating explications to some terminal point preassessed as sufficient, refers to the completeness vs. the incompleteness of the range of denotative (specified) meaning of a term. The second problem, the residue of meaning of an explicated term, refers to the completeness vs. the incompleteness of the range of connotative (specifiable) meaning of a term. Whereas the former is resolved by reference to the criterion of empirical utility, the latter is resolved by reference to both empirical utility and theoretical fertility, as these are partially determined by the level of semantic precision of the particular sociological term(s) under consideration. In other words, the specification of the semantic status of the residue of meaning in an explicated sociological term must be accomplished by determining the level of precision of usage that can be tolerated, which, in turn, requires an examination of the overall yield of empirical utility and theoretical fertility from the term in question.

Sociology has yet to develop requisite predictive statements whereby the yield of empirical utility and theoretical fertility from its terms can be ascertained. Because of this shortcoming, the exact mechanics of accomplishing the objective will include the formation of a set of statements that will specify how the explicated term is to be used (i.e., what general types of theoretical predictive statements will it be embedded in, what will be its function in these statements, etc.) and what relation its explicated meaning will have to its residue of meaning (i.e., what are the necessary and sufficient conditions for the application of the term to those empirical situations to which it may apply).

THE PROBLEMATIC ASSUMED LEGITIMACY OF THE TERM
TO BE EXPLICATED

Dumont and Wilson accurately point out the assumption that is involved in the explication of sociological terms. They assert that they are "developing a practical program for selecting or developing those aspects of current sociological theory that show promise for eventual conformity with these criteria [that permit the construction of definitive theories in sociology]" (1967: 986). How one goes about assessing the "promissory status" or "potential significance" of a particular sociological term becomes problematic. The only possible way of doing this is to assume that a given term has such "status or significance." They attempt to sugarcoat this assumption first by positing such things as "implicit theories" and "theory sketches," which may implicitly convey such status or significance to seemingly "isolated abstract concepts," or nonsignificant sociological terms, and second by asserting that the decision as to whether or not a given sociological term is to be afforded such status of significance is based exclusively on "methodological" grounds. But they never clearly specify what they mean by "methodological grounds," and this statement in no way makes clear exactly what the final decision is to be based upon. The closest they get to so doing is by example:

For example, although there is no explicit theory or theory sketch [less formalized explicit theory] of social stratification, researchers in the area seem generally agreed as to the importance of the term 'social status', and implementations of this concept in actual research situations suggest its candidacy for lower-order theoretical language in any theoretical undertaking. [p. 990]

So it becomes clear that, despite all the sugarcoating, this decision is based on the amount of agreement among those researchers using the term as to its importance and the frequency with which the term is used in research. This is equivalent to saying that a particular sociological term is afforded "promissory status" or "potential significance" because it is assumed to have such status or significance by those who use it. Of course, this is not to deny that there may be some preliminary evidence upon which the decision may have been based. The term may have been used in unexplicated form in previous research or may be the topic of concern for certain researchers, etc. But the fact remains that one chooses to explicate a given term because he assumes that in its explicated form that term will permit the formulation of definitive theoretical statements, or (in Hempel's terms) "the development of a comprehensive, rigorous, and sound theoretical system" (1952: 12).

This assumption is problematic insofar as the explicated term cannot be rendered precise enough to be a candidate for a given theoretical system. Or, to put it differently, this assumption may attribute a greater level of precision to the explicated term than that term can ever approximate: the term may never have enough precision to be usable in a theoretical language system. This may be the case for any number of reasons. The term may have been used opaquely in a low precision language system prior to explication. By explicating it, then, one assumes that it designates observable phenomena at the terminal point of explication, when it probably does not. This may very well be the case with most sociological terms, given their equivalence in precision of usage to a conventional language system and given all the language problems that this implies. Similarly a particular term may be too vague, ambiguous, or contradictory to permit explication precise enough to warrant giving it candidacy for a theoretical language system. This can be true despite assumptions to the contrary. For example, "social system" may be so vague that its residue of meaning is an insurmountable problem.

The crux of this problem for explication is that terms which either should not or cannot be explicated are still eligible for explication given the assumption of their "status or significance." There are no rules of explication, therefore, that act as potential corrective devices when the particular term to be explicated suffers from any of the general language problems mentioned in Chapters 2 and 3. This is particularly troublesome for sociology because of the extent to which its core terminology is subject to these problems.

EXPLICATION PLUS SYSTEMATIZATION:
A MORE COMPREHENSIVE SOLUTION?

One may legitimately ask, if these techniques of systematization and explication in sociology were used in a complementary fashion, then would sociologists have a more comprehensive solution for their theoretical-definitional problems? The solution would be more comprehensive in the sense that sociologists employing these techniques in combination would be getting at the root causes of more of their problems than if they employed either technique alone. But such a solution would be neither complete nor sufficient because of some of the problems that even a combination of both approaches would necessarily overlook. The basic difficulty with both explication and systematization as they are used in sociology is that they presume the pre-existence of a sociological language system which is at least adequate. Moreover, neither technique addresses itself to the question of predictive error resulting from this faulty language system. The most important questions would remain unanswered.

SUMMARY

Four basic difficulties impede the utility of explication as a language control device in sociology. First, the predicates that explicate a particular term are themselves subject to explication of infinite regress. Second, most sociological terms are so vague and have acquired so much "meaning" that any one instance of explication may fail to deal adequately with the problem of a confusing "residue of meaning" that exists apart from the explicated meaning of the term. Third, the very explication of a term assumes the legitimacy of the term in the sense that it assumes that the term has "promissory status" or "potential significance" as a member of a definitive theoretical system. This assumption becomes problematic when there is actually an unbridgeable disparity between the real and the assumed levels of precision of the term. Fourth, even given the ideal case of explication, it of necessity suffers from being just one way in which the level of precision of a language system can be increased: i.e., it deals with only one factor that contributes to the level of precision of a given language system.

Although explication and systematization can be used jointly to good effect, there are still limits on the benefits to be derived from such an approach. This results from two factors. First, both presume the pre-existence of an adequate sociological language system. Second, neither approach deals with this problematic language system and its maintenance of high levels of predictive error.

Exchange Theory and Ethnomethodology: The Appeal to Observables

It has been implicit and explicit in the preceding criticisms of sociology that the only true answer for its theoretical problems is intensive research into limited domains of inquiry with sufficient reference to observable human-behavioral events. In the last decade two loosely knit "schools" of sociology have swung the focus from macro-level survey research to micro-level observational and experimental research dealing with class 1 phenomena. These are the exchange theorists and the ethnomethodologists. Homans (1961), Blau (1964), Lévi-Strauss (1957), and Gouldner (1960) have contributed greatly to exchange theory, while Goffman (1961; 1967), Garfinkel (1967), and Becker (1960) have contributed to ethnomethodology. These lists are not exhaustive, and the categories themselves are heuristic. They are being used to refer to two trends in sociology with the same outcome—the appeal to observable behavior.

Briefly, both ethnomethodologists and exchange theorists are concerned with the same basic model of social behavior: Actor A does (or presents stimuli) X, Y, or Z, to which actor B responds by doing (or presenting stimuli) U, V, or W. This model is elaborated by the specification of situational components: e.g., actor A does X at $T_1 \ldots _n$ in situation S_1, to which actor B responds by doing U. Of course, this action-reaction sequence is only a kernel sequence in a pattern that is modified according to the intentions and objectives of the theorist.

There are important differences between exchange theorists and ethnomethodologists, however. The former have as their explicit purpose the explanation of selected aspects of this basic model and its elaborations. They are concerned with definition, predictive form, and deductive explanation. Ethnomethodologists, on the other hand, are less concerned with such formal matters. They are satisfied with describing certain recurrences within the context of the basic model. Their approach does yield predictions and explanations, but, with a few notable exceptions, these must be extrapolated or interpolated from their work.

The explanatory medium for all exchange theorists is the economic or behavioristic analogy. Thus, Blau analyzes the action-reaction sequence as an exchange in which actor A does something that increases the rewards or costs of what actor B does. Homans analyzes this sequence in a similar fashion but ties his efforts in with the operant conditioning techniques of B. F. Skinner, utilizing the famous law of effect. Generally, the descriptive as well as the (implicitly) explanatory medium of ethnomenthodology is the game analogy. Both actors in a sequence are constantly referred to as game players whose actions are governed by certain discoverable rules of play. Actions and reactions are therefore viewed as probabilistic events, whose likelihood of occurrence depends upon the format of the particular game situation and the rules that define that situation. It should be emphasized that this model is used loosely by ethnomethodologists to give some orientation to their work. They rarely employ it with the degree of rigor customary among the mathematical game theorists (see Luce and Raiffa, 1957).

PROBLEMS WITH EXCHANGE THEORY AND ETHNOMETHODOLOGY

Both approaches are only general orientations: they direct the researcher's attention to observable human behavior without systematically and rigorously dealing with the phenomena. This is most notable in their general failure to generate original or systematically codified data. The data referred to are either borrowed from other sociologists or relevant researchers and are loosely described rather than systematically presented and analyzed, or they are descriptive and intuitive to begin with and are expressed in conventional or traditional sociological language. For example, Homans refers to the Skinner's work and cites his own (1950) reanalysis of prior sociological studies without mentioning the extensive problems of either. While Goffman declares that the work in his area is closely related to and supported by the work done on animal communication, he does not even cite specific references.

These calls to observables, then, have a hollow ring. This is confirmed by their extensive use of problematic sociological terminology. Thus, terms like "society," "rights," "obligations," "legitimacy," "power," "values," "social processes," "social structure," "group," "activity," "approval," "enemy," "culture," "institution," "informal vs. formal group," "roles," "rules," "play," "integration," "differentiation," "position," "status," "order," "organization," "sanctioned relationship," "social affects," "interaction," etc. are used extensively in both approaches, with the concomitant problems of ambiguity, vagueness, opacity, and contradiction that they imply. Moreover, despite the emphasis on "good" definition by the exchange theorists, the definitions employed are problematic, not only in the sense that they are ambiguous, vague, opaque, or contradictory, but also in the sense that they are used inappropriately: nominal and ostensive definition are used to legitimate problematic terms; primitives are improperly used; the completeness assumption is utilized to introduce problematic terms into the language system; and no disposition concepts are employed to designate action referents. Finally, the systematizing technique employed is conventional grammar, and the predictions that are specified are of the lowest level of precision, with all the resulting problems that this implies.

THE ANALYSIS OF VERBAL BEHAVIOR: AN ILLUSTRATION

To confirm the fact that these difficulties arise in both exchange theory and ethnomethodology, one need only extend the arguments set forth in the preceding chapters. Rather than give specific examples, I shall mention one area in which they are most easily observed, both because of their salience and because of the existence of more precise, nonsociological research as a base line for comparison.

As was mentioned in Chapter 3, one of the crucial omissions from sociological theory language is an adequate set of terms and defining object predicates that designate verbal behavior. The shift in focus of both the exchange theorists and ethnomethodologists to observable human behavior would presumably correct this to some degree. This should be particularly true of the ethnomethodologists, given their professed interest in verbal behavioral phenomena and in communication in general. Interestingly enough, however, this is not the case.

These theorists do call attention to the importance of dealing with verbal behavior and other communication phenomena, but they persist in relying heavily on inference, subjective impression, and group terminology in describing these events. The end result is the initial development of a problematic language system to deal with this domain of interest.

The most fundamental difficulty with this infant language system is its failure to assign reliable spatio-temporal referents to verbal phenomena. Thus, the exchange theorists refer to such abstract entities as "verbal approval" for reward, "verbal chastisement" for punishment, and "verbal directions, requests, and commands" for stimuli without supplying sufficient information to assign reliable spatio-temporal referents to particular verbal behaviors. And the ethnomethodologists speak of "verbal interaction," "indexical expressions," "objective expressions," "talk," "salutations," "avoidance rituals," etc., again without sufficient information to assign reliable spatio-temporal referents to particular instances of these communicational phenomena. (Chomsky, 1959, has presented a classic critique of the extrapolation of operant conditioning principles to explain verbal behavior generally. His chief argument involves the insufficient specification of empirical referents for the terms employed.) This serious failing is in sharp contrast to comparable research efforts by psycholinguists, linguists, and those assorted professionals dealing with animal and human communication (for example, see Dixon and Horton, 1968; Sebeok, 1968; Jakabovits and Miron, 1967; Chomsky, 1965; Fodor and Katz, 1968; Naess, 1953; and Salzinger and Salzinger, 1967). Generally, the rapidly developing body of research applies the appropriate research strategy to limited sets of phenomena while observing the rules of good theory construction. It is noteworthy that the ethnomethodologists do not even refer specifically to any of these research endeavors despite the avowed relevance of such endeavors to their work (see Goffman 1967: 1). This is but another manifestation of the insulation of sociologists from relevant empirical research, due to the bias of the discipline that maintains a mythical demarcation between theory and research.

It is apparent, then, that the exchange theorists and ethnomethodologists are prone to make the same mistakes as traditional sociological theorists. Their theory language is subject to the same language problems and failure to control adequately for these problems. Furthermore, their terms do not sufficiently designate observable phenomena, and their predictions are of the least precise form.

Despite all these faults, their work can be considered a partial solution to the problems plaguing traditional sociology because they do attempt to shift the focus of sociology to observable phenomena. This is but a first step that must be accompanied by other changes if a complete solution to these problems is ever to be attained.

Conclusion of the Book

The complete solution to sociological language problems has been implicit in the criticisms appearing throughout the book. Sociologists must be more concerned with the referential meanings of their terms. They must use explicit and rigorous definitions. They must formulate disposition concepts and definitions while using the most appropriate predictive form. Furthermore, they cannot be satisfied with conventional grammar as their systematizing device; they must express their theoretical statements in more precise form. This does *not* imply that sociological explanations must be deductive, for the requirements of deductive explanation may be too severe for sociology at this early stage in its development. Entirely too much time and energy have been expended by sociologists in working out deductive explanations that have too small a yield in empirical utility.

These demands, in turn, imply a whole new research strategy for sociologists. The appeal to sociologists to deal with observable phenomena and with explicit spatio-temporal referents, rather than with reports about these phenomena, is an emphatic one. Its empirical restrictions are not to be denied, nor can they be circumvented by the construction of problematic descriptions of these phenomena in the style of exchange theorists and ethnomethodologists. At the minimum, these restrictions require a reliable inter- and intraresearch certification of the existence of the human behavioral objects, properties, or relations that are either directly or indirectly referred to by sociological terms. This, in turn, requires the reliable observation of these empirical events through time by one or more observers, as well as between observers agreement as to the occurrence, nonoccurrence, or degrees of occurrence of these events.

Beyond fulfilling these requirements, the exact investigative technique employed can and will vary. But the necessity for replication is unvarying. Sociologists must map out limited empirical domains by whatever criteria they wish: the possible criteria range from self-interest to studying phenomena because one is told to do so. They must constantly shuttle back and forth from these domains to their symbolic reconstructions of them, whether they are conducting initial investigations of the particular empirical phenomena or testing sophisticated hypotheses developed after years of research. Replication and repetition are the cornerstones of any science.

THE VALUE OF SOCIOLOGY

Some would question whether sociology should aspire to scientific status. I have tried here to demonstrate that sociology is *not* a science and to state the reasons for its failure. I mean, however, to affirm the fruitfulness of scientific stature for sociology. By attaining this goal, sociology will provide the information about human social behavior that is so crucially needed at this point in history. It may very well supply the knowledge necessary for man's future survival. Sociology asks the right questions; it is time that sociology began supplying the right answers.

Selected Bibliography

Abel, T. 1948. "The operation called 'Verstehen,'" *American Journal of Sociology*, 54: 211–18.

Adams, S. 1953. "Status incongruence as a variable in small group performance," *Social Forces*, 32: 16–22.

Argyris, C. 1956. *Diagnosing Human Relations in Organizations: A Case Study of a Hospital*. New Haven: Yale University Labor & Management Center.

Bar-Hillel, V. 1960. "On recursive definition of empirical sciences," *Proceedings of the XIth International Congress of Philosophy*, 5: 160–65.

Bar-Hillel, V. 1964. *Language and Information: Selected Essays on Their Theory and Interaction*. Reading, Mass.: Addison-Wesley; and Jerusalem: Jerusalem Press.

Bateman, J. and H. W. Dunham 1948. "The state mental hospital as a specialized community experience," *American Journal of Psychiatry*, 55: 445–49.

Bateson, G., D. Jackson and J. Haley. 1956. "Toward a theory of schizophrenia," *Behavioral Science*, 1: 251–64.

Barker, R. G. 1968. *Ecological Psychology*. Stanford: Stanford University Press.

Beck, L. W. 1953. "Constructions and inferred entities," in H. Feigl and M. Brodbeck, eds., *Readings in the Philosophy of Science*. New York: Appleton-Century-Crofts.

Becker, H. S. 1960. "Notes on the concept of commitment," *American Journal of Sociology*, 66: 32–40.

Benoit-Smullyan. 1944. "Status, status types and status interrelations," *American Sociological Review*, 9: 151–59.

Bergman, A. 1956. "Sense and nonsense in operationism," in P. Frank, ed., *The Validation of Scientific Theories*. Boston: The Beacon Press.

Berko, Jr. 1961. "The child's learning of English Morphology," in S. Saporta, ed., *Psycholinguistics, a Book of Readings*. New York: Holt, Rinehart and Winston.

Berlo, D. K. 1960. *The Process of Communcation: an Introduction to Theory and Practice*. New York: Holt, Rinehart and Winston.

Bierstedt, R. 1959. "Nominal and real definitions in sociological theory," in L. Gross, ed., *Symposium on Sociological Theory*. White Plains, N.Y.: Row, Peterson.

Bijou, S. and D. Baer. 1961. *Child Development*. Vol. I. New York: Appleton-Century-Crofts.

Bijou, S., R. Peterson, and M. Ault 1968. "A method of integrate descriptive and experimental field studies at the level of data and empirical concepts," *Journal of Applied Behavior Analysis*, 1: 175–91.

Blalock, H. M. 1964. *Causal Inferences in Nonexperimental Research*. Chapel Hill: University of North Carolina Press.

Blalock, H. M. 1967a. *Toward a Theory of Minority-Group Relations*. New York: Wiley.

Blalock, H. M. 1967b. "Status inconsistency and interaction: some alternative models," *American Journal of Sociology*, 72: 305–15.

Blalock, H. M. 1968. "The measurement problem: a gap between the language of theory and research," in H. M. Blalock and A. B. Blalock, eds., *Methodology in Social Research*. New York: McGraw-Hill.

Blalock, H. M. 1969. *Theory Construction: from Verbal to Mathematical Formulations*. Englewood Cliffs: Prentice-Hall.

Blau, P. M. 1964. *Exchange and Power in Social Life*. New York: Wiley.

Blau, P. M. 1970. "A formal theory of differentiation in organizations," *Americal Sociological Review*, 35: 201–18.

Blau, P. M., and R. W. Scott. 1962. *Formal Organization: A Comparative Approach*. San Francisco: Chandler.

Bloom, S. M. 1963. *The Doctor and his Patient*. New York: Russell Sage.

Blumer, H. 1954. "What is wrong with social theory?" *American Sociological Review*, 19: 3–10.

Brandon, A. 1965. "Status congruence and expectation," *Sociometry*, 28: 272–88.

Brannon, A. B. 1947. "The social structure of a criminal unit of a psychiatric hospital," in R. Linder and R. Selinger, eds., *The Handbook of Correctional Psychology*. New York: The Philosophical Library.

Bridgemen, P. W. 1927. *The Logic of Modern Physics*. New York: Macmillan.

Brodbeck, May. 1958. "Methodological individualism: definition and reduction," *Philosophy of Science*, 25: 9–17.

Broom, L., and P. Selznick. 1968. *Sociology: A Text with Adapted Readings*. New York: Harper and Row.

Brown, R. 1958. *Words and Things*. Glencoe, Ill.: The Free Press.

Brown, R. 1965. *Social Psychology*. New York: The Free Press.

Burgess, R. L. and D. Bushell. 1969. *Behavioral Sociology*. New York: Columbia University Press.

Campbell, D. T., and J. C. Stanley. 1963. *Experimental and Quasi-Experimental Designs for Research*. Chicago: Rand McNally.

Carnap, R. 1942. *Introduction to Semantics*. Cambridge, Mass.: Harvard University Press.

Carnap, R. 1953. "Testability and meaning," In H. Feigl and May Brodbeck, eds., *Readings in the Philosophy of Science*. New York: Appleton-Century-Crofts.

Carnap, R. 1956. "The methodological character of theoretical concepts," in H. Feigl and M. Scriven, eds., Minnesota Studies in the Philosophy of Science, Vol. I. *The Foundations of Science and the Concepts of Psychology and Psychoanalysis*. Minneapolis: University of Minnesota Press.

Carroll, J. B. 1964. *Language and Thought*. Englewood Cliffs, N.J.: Prentice-Hall.

Caudill, W. 1958. *The Psychiatric Hospital as a Small Society*. Cambridge, Mass.: Harvard University Press.

Cherry, C. 1957. *On Human Communications*. New York: M. I. T. Press and Wiley.

Chomsky, N. 1957. *Syntactic Structures*. The Hague: Mouton.

Chomsky, N. 1959. "Verbal behavior (a review)," *Language*, 35: 26–58.

Chomsky, N. 1965. *Aspects of the Theory of Syntax*. Cambridge, Mass.: M. I. T. Press.

Cohen, M. R. and E. Nagel. 1934. *An Introduction to Logic and Scientific Method*. New York: Harcourt, Brace and World.

Costner, H. L. and R. K. Leik. 1964. "Deductions from axiomatic theory," *American Sociological Review*, 29: 819–35.

Cottrell, L. 1942a. "The analysis of situational field in social psychology," *American Sociological Review*, 7: 370–82.

Cottrell, L. 1942b. "The adjustment of an individual to his age and sex role." *American Sociological Review*, 7: 617–20.

Cronbach, L. J. 1957. "The two disciplines of scientific psychology," *American Psychologist*, 12: 670–84.

Deese, J. 1961. "From the isolated verbal unit to connected discourse," in C. Cofer and B. Musgrave, eds., *Verbal Learning and Verbal Behavior*. New York: McGraw-Hill.

DeSoto, C. B. 1960. "Learning a social structure," *Journal of Abnormal and Social Psychology*, 60: 417–21.

Devereux, G. 1944. "The social structure of a schizophrenic ward and its therapeutic fitness," *Journal of Clinical Psychopathology*, 6: 231–65.

Devereux, G. 1949. "The social structure of the hospital as a factor in total therapy," *American Journal of Orthopsychiatry*, 19: 492–500.

Dingle, H. 1965. Introduction, in H. Bergson, *Duration and Simultaneity*. New York: Bobbs-Merrill.

Dixon, T. R. and D. L. Horton, eds. *Verbal Behavior and General Behavior Theory*. Englewood Cliffs, N.J.: Prentice-Hall.

Dulany, D. 1962. "The place of hypotheses and intentions—an analysis of verbal control in verbal conditioning," *Journal of Personality*, 30: 102–29.

Dumont, R. G. and W. J. Wilson. 1967. "Aspects of concept formation, explication, and theory construction in sociology," *American Sociological Review*, 32: 985–95.

Dunham, W. H. and S. K. Weinberg. 1960. *The Culture of the State Mental Hospital*. Detroit: Wayne State University Press.

Durkheim, E. 1958. *The Rules of Sociological Method*. Glencoe, Ill.: The Free Press.

Epstein, W. 1961. "Influence of syntactical structure on learning," *American Journal of Psychiaty*. 74: 80–85.

Exline, R. V. and R. C. Zeller. 1959. "Status congruence and interpersonal conflict in decision-making groups, *Human Relations*, 12: 147–62.

Fiedler, F. E. and W. A. Meuwese. 1965. "Leader's contribution to task performance in cohesive and uncohesive groups," *Journal of Abnormal and Social Psychology*, 67: 83–87.

Fonseca, O. W. 1956. "Emergent social structure among short-term psychiatric patients," *International Journal of Social Psychiatry*, 2: 132–41.

Fodor, J. A. and J. J. Katz. 1968. *The Structure of Language: Readings in the Philosophy of Language*. Englewood Cliffs, N.J.: Prentice-Hall.

Garfinkel, H. 1967. *Studies in Ethnomethodology*. Englewood Cliffs, N.J.: Prentice-Hall.

Goffman, E. 1957. "Status consistency and preference for change in power distribution," *American Sociological Review*, 22: 275–81.

Goffman, E. 1961. *Encounters*. Indianapolis: Bobbs-Merrill.

Goffman, E. 1967. *Interaction Ritual*. New York: Doubleday.

Goodman, M. and W. V. Quine. 1947. "Steps toward a constructive nominalism," *Journal of Symbolic Logic*. 12: 105–22.

Gouldner, A. 1960. "The norm of reciprocity," *American Sociological Review*, 25: 161–78.

Green, A. W. 1960. *Sociology: an Analysis of Life in Modern Society*. 3d ed. New York: McGraw-Hill.

Gross, L. 1959. "Theory construction in sociology: a methodological inquiry," in L. Gross, ed., *Symposium on Sociological Theory*. White Plains, N.Y.: Row, Peterson.

Hanna, J. R. 1968. "An explication of 'explication,' " *Philosophy of Science*, 35: 28–44.

Hempel, C. G. 1952. *Foundations of Concept Formation in Empirical Science*. Chicago: University of Chicago Press.

Hempel, C. G. 1956. "A logical appraisal of operationism," in P. Frank, ed., *The Validation of Scientific Theories*. Boston: The Beacon Press.

Hempel, C. G. 1958. "The theoretician's dilemma: a study in the logic of theory construction," in H. Feigl., M. Scriven, and G. Maxwell, eds., Minnesota Studies in the Philosophy of Science, Vol. II. *Theories and the Mind-body Problem*. Minneapolis: University of Minnesota Press.

Homans, G. C. 1950. *The Human Group*. New York: Harcourt, Brace.

Homans, G. C. 1961. *The Elementary Forms of Social Behavior*. New York: Harcourt, Brace and World.

Homans, G. C. 1964. "Contemporary theory in sociology," in R. E. L. Faris, ed., *Handbook of Modern Sociology*. Chicago: Rand McNally.

Homans, G. C. 1967. "Fundamental social process," in H. J. Smelser, ed., *Sociology: An Introduction*. New York: Wiley.

Howes, D. and C. E. Osgood. 1954. "On the combination of associative probabilities in linguistic contexts," *American Journal of Psychology*, 67: 241–58.

Hume, D. 1946. *An Enquiry Concerning Human Understanding*. La Salle, Ill.: Open Court.

Inkeles, A. 1964. *What is Sociology?* Englewood Cliffs, N.J.: Prentice-Hall.

Jackson, E. 1962. "Status inconsistency and symptoms of stress," *American Sociological Review*, 27: 469–80.

Jacobovits, L. A. and M. S. Miron, eds. 1967. *Readings in the Philosophy of Language*. Englewood Cliffs, N.J.: Prentice-Hall.

Kadushin, C. 1968. "Power, influence and social circles," *American Sociological Review*, 33: 685–99.

Kaplan, A. 1946. "Definition and specification of meaning," *Journal of Philosophy*, 43: 281–88.

Kaplan, A. 1964. *The Conduct of Inquiry*. San Francisco: Chandler.

Katz, J. J. 1964a. "Semi-sentences," in J. A. Fodor and J. J. Katz, eds., *The Structure of Language: Readings in the Philosophy of Language*. Englewood Cliffs, N.J.: Prentice-Hall.

Katz, J. J. 1964b. "Analyticity and contradiction in natural language," *Ibid.*, pp. 519–43.

Katz, J. J., and J. A. Fodor. 1964. "The structure of a semantic theory," *Ibid.*, pp. 479–518.

Kemeny, D. G. 1959. *A Philosopher Looks at Science*. New York: Van Nostrand.

Kemeny, J. G. and P. Oppenheim. 1956. "On reduction," *Philosophical Studies*, Jan.–Feb.

Kimberly, J. C. 1967. "Status inconsistency: a reformulation of a theoretical problem," *Human Relations*, 27: 469–80.

Kimberly, J. C. and P. V. Crosbie. 1967. "An experimental test of a reward-cost formulation of status inconsistency," *Journal of Experimental Social Psychology*, 3: 399–415.

Krasner, L. 1958. "Studies of the conditioning of verbal behavior," *Psychological Bulletin*, 55: 148–70.

Kroeber, A. L. and C. Kluckhohn. 1952. *Culture: A Critical Review of Concepts and Definitions*. Cambridge, Mass.: the Museum.

Lachenmeyer, C. 1969. "The language of literature: a conceptual reanalysis," *Linguistics*, 55: 32–47.

Lachenmeyer, C. 1970. "A note on the existence of social systems," *Sociology and Social Research*, 55: 102–108.

La Piere, R. T. 1965. *Social Change*. New York: McGraw-Hill.

Lenski, G. 1954. "Status crystallization, a non-vertical dimension of social status," *American Sociological Review*. 19: 504–13.

Lenski, G. 1956. "Status crystallization, withdrawal from participation in voluntary groups," *American Sociological Review*, 21: 458–64.

Lewis, G. I. 1952. "The modes of meaning," in L. Linsky, ed., *Semantics and the Philosophy of Language*. Urbana: University of Illinois Press.

Lévi-Strauss, C. 1957. "The principle of reciprocity," in L. A. Cosar and B. Rosenberg, *Sociological Theory*. New York: Macmillan.

Lounsbury, F. G. 1963. "Linguistics and psychology," in S. Koch, ed., *Psychology, A Study in Science*. Vol. 6. New York: McGraw-Hill.

Luce, D. R. and H. Raiffa. 1957. *Games and Decisions*. New York: Wiley.

MacCorquodale, K. and P. E. Meehl. 1948. "On a distinction between hypothetical constructs and intervening variables," *Psychological Review*, 55: 95–107.

McFarland, D. D. 1970. "Review of H. M. Blalock, Jr., Theory Construction: From Verbal to Mathematical Formulations," *Social Forces*, 48: 543–44.

Maier, N. 1949. *Frustration and the Study of Behavior without a Goal*. New York: McGraw-Hill.

Margenau, H. 1950. *The Nature of Physical Reality*. New York: McGraw-Hill.

Martin, B. 1963. "Reward and punishment associated with the same goal response, a factor in the learning of motives," *Psychological Bulletin*, 60: 441–51.

Merton, R. K. 1957. *Social Theory and Social Structure*. Glencoe, Ill.: The Free Press.

Merton, R. K. and R. A. Nisbet. 1966. *Contemporary Social Problems*. New York: Harcourt, Brace and World.

Miller, G. A. 1962. "Some psychological studies of grammar," *American Psychologist*, 17: 748–62.

Miller, G. A. 1967. *The Psychology of Communication*. New York: Basic Books.

Morris, C. W. 1946. *Signs, Language and Behavior*. New York: Prentice-Hall.

Mowrer, O. H. 1960. *Learning Theory and the Symbolic Process*. New York: Wiley.

Naess, A. 1952. "Toward a theory of interpretation and preciseness," in L. Linsky, ed., *Semantics and the Philosophy of Language*. Urbana: University of Illinois Press.

Naess, A. 1953. *Interpretation and Preciseness, a Contribution to the Theory of Communication*. Oslo: Ikommisjon Hos Jaeob Djbwad.

Nagel, E. 1953. "The meaning of reduction in the natural sciences," in P. Wiener, ed., *Readings in the Philosophy of Science*. New York: Scribner.

Nagel, E. 1961. *The Structure of Science*. New York: Harcourt, Brace & World. Chapters 13 and 14, pp. 450–56.

Noble, C. E. 1952. "An analysis of meaning," *Psychological Review*, 59: 421–30.

Northrop, F. 1947. *The Logic of the Sciences and Humanities*. New York: Macmillan.

Osgood, C. E., G. J. Suci, and P. H. Tannenbaum. 1957. *The Measurement of Meaning*. Urbana: University of Illinois Press.

Osgood, C. E. 1963. "On understanding and creating sentences," *American Psychologist*, 18: 735–51.

Pellegrin, R. V. and F. L. Bates. 1959. "Congruity and incongruity of status attributes," *Social Forces*, 38: 23–28.
Ploch, D. R. 1970. "Theorizing and statistics," *American Sociologist*, 5: 143–46.
Quine, W. V. 1951. *Mathematical Logic*. New York: Harper & Row.
Quine, W. V. 1960. *World and Object*. New York: M. I. T. Press and Wiley.
Riesman, D. 1961. *The Lonely Crowd*. New Haven: Yale University Press.
Ryle, G. 1960. "Systematically misleading expressions," in A. G. H. Flew, ed., *Logic and Language—First Series*. Oxford: Basil Blackwell.
Salzinger, K. and S. Salzinger. 1967. *Research in Verbal Behavior and Some Neurophysiological Implications*. New York: Academic Press.
Sampson, E. E. 1963. "Status congruence and cognitive consistency," *Sociometry*, 26: 146–61.
Schuham, A. I. 1967. "The double-bind hypothesis a decade later," *Psychological Bulletin*, 68: 409–16.
Scriven, M. S. 1956a. "A study of radical behaviorism," in H. Feigel and M. Scriven, eds., Minnesota Studies in the Philosophy of Science, Vol. I. *The Foundations of Science and the Concepts of Psychology and Psychoanalysis*. Minneapolis: University of Minnesota Press.
Scriven, M. S. 1956b. "A possible distinction between traditional disciplines and the study of human behavior," *Ibid.*, pp. 330–39.
Scriven, M. S. 1958. "Definitions, explanations, and theories," in H. Feigl, M. Scriven, and G. Maxwell, eds., Minnesota Studies in the Philosophy of Science, Vol. II. *Theories and the Mind-body Problem*. Minneapolis: University of Minnesota Press.
Sebeok, T. A. ed., 1968. *Animal Communication*. Bloomingdale: Indiana University Press.
Secord, P. F. and C. W. Backman. 1964. *Social Psychology*. New York: McGraw-Hill.
Sidman, M. 1960. *Tactics of Scientific Research*. New York: Basic Books.
Simmel, G. 1950. *The Sociology of G. Simmel*. Translated, edited, and with an introduction by Kurt H. Wolff. Glencoe, Ill.: The Free Press.
Simon, H. A. 1957. *Models of Man*. New York: Wiley.
Skinner, B. F. 1953. *Science and Human Behavior*. New York: Macmillan.
Skinner, B. F. 1957. *Verbal Behavior*. New York: Appleton-Century-Crofts.
Smelser, W. T. 1961. "Dominance as a factor in achievement and perception in cooperative problem solving interactions," *Journal of Abnormal and Social Psychology*, 62: 535–42.
Timasheff, N. B. 1957. *Sociological Theory: Its Nature and Growth*. New York: Random House.
Ullman, S. 1962. *Semantics, an Introduction to the Science of Meaning*. New York: Barnes & Noble.
Watzlawick, P., J. Beavin, and D. D. Jackson. 1967. *Pragmatics of Human Communication: A Study of Interactional Patterns, Pathologies, and Paradoxes*. New York: W. W. Norton.
Weber, M. 1962a. *Basic Concepts in Sociology*. Translated and with an introduction by H. P. Secher. New York: Philosophical Library.

Weber, M. 1962b. *From Max Weber: Essays in Sociology.* Translated by M. H. Gerth & C. Wright Mills. New York: Oxford University Press.

Wender, P. H. 1967. "Communicative unclarity: some comments on the rhetoric of confusion," *Psychiatry*, 30: 332–49.

Willer, D., and M. Webster. 1970. "Theoretical concepts and observables," *American Sociological Review.* 35: 748–56.

Zetterberg, H. 1954 (1st ed.) and 1965 (3d ed.). *On Theory and Verification in Sociology*, London: Bedminster Press.

Author Index

Subject Index

DATE DUE
